Laughing with My Mouth Full

Pam Freir

Laughing with My Mouth Full

Tales from a Gulf Islands Kitchen

HarperCollins*PublishersLtd*

Pam Freir gratefully acknowledges the assistance of the Canada Council
for the Arts and the British Columbia Arts Council.

Pages 259–260 constitute a continuation of the copyright page.

HarperCollins books may be purchased for educational, business,
or sales promotional use through our Special Markets Department.

HarperCollins Publishers Ltd
2 Bloor Street East, 20th Floor
Toronto, Ontario, Canada
M4W 1A8

www.harpercollins.ca

Library and Archives Canada Cataloguing in Publication

Freir, Pam
Laughing with my mouth full : tales from a Gulf Islands kitchen / Pam Freir.

ISBN-13: 978-0-00-200801-3
ISBN-10: 0-00-200801-7

1. Freir, Pam. 2. Food – Humor. 3. Cookery – Humor.
4. Food writers – British Columbia – Biography. I. Title.

TX649.F73A3 2005   641.3'092   C2005-902408-9

HC 9 8 7 6 5 4 3 2 1

Printed and bound in the United States
Set in Candida and Monotype Plantin

To Chris, with love and gratitude

Contents

1. Open Wide

A food lover's life, in a nutshell, from a Nova Scotia childhood to island living, West Coast–style, today. Breakfast with Grandad, Devon cream teas, warm gingerbread and pizza—I savour it all, learning as I go, and marry a man who was traumatized by a fondue

2. From Where I Sit

I trade the glitz of the city for a rainforest hideaway and discover the down-to-earth goodness of real food. I drink wild tea under the cedars; I chat with chickens; I forage for fiddleheads, celebrate spring in a nettle patch and serve breakfast, non-stop, to the houseguests from Hell

3. Who's That Klutz in My Kitchen?

I attempt to braid garlic and fail. I try peeling beets and fail. I concoct an improbable ragù and salute the books that whetted my appetite for life beyond Hamburger Helper. I puzzle over the dumb things that happen to smart people as I Windex my bread, host the first annual Cornish hen stuffathon and wash another batch of cookies down the drain

4. Tomorrow We May Diet

Some thoughts on the virtues of wine and weight-loss avoidance as I learn how to plump myself up, eat like a mouse and pretend that cholesterol doesn't count

5. Yuck! That's Offal!

I boil up a big grey tongue, assemble a haggis and explore a host of culinary oddities from Marmite and muesli to frog-spawn pudding and bird's nest soup

6. People and Other Mealtime Curiosities

I read corn cobs, brush up on my table manners and contemplate the curious, ages-old bond between man and his barbeque. I raise the subject of sex at the dinner table and manage, against all odds, to survive several meals with small children

7. Desperate Measures

Some thoughts on stuffing a camel, cooking with Google, re-inventing the bouillabaisse and mastering the feng shui of refrigerator management. I also battle a hangover, dine in the dark and wrestle an artichoke in public with disappointing results

8. Travels with My Tummy

I'm on the road—roughing it in Bummer's Flats, exploring beach-shack cuisine in the Dominican Republic, conversing in Spanish with a chef with twelve toes and dining on lobster under the watchful eye of the U.S. Secret Service

Introduction

I frequently need reminding that, for many people, food is not the undiluted pleasure that it is for me. For some—the anxious host, the busy chef, the glutton at the sushi bar—food is a serious business indeed. For others, it is solace, nourishing some hunger that life has failed to feed. And for far too many, it is just another bit of bother in a too-short, crowded day.

Then there's me, ever grateful for what I regard as one of life's most delicious pleasures. And not only that, I get to write about it, a delightful preoccupation for which only the most modest of credentials are required. I'm not a scholar. I'm certainly no gourmet. I'm not even a particularly accomplished cook: I can make a cookie stick where no cookie's ever stuck before. I have trouble peeling beets. But, baffling though food sometimes is, I love my grub. So what if my soufflé sags and onions make me burp? Food is fun. And writing about it is, in part at least, bred in the bone.

When I was a child, adults would ask, as adults are wont to do, "When you grow up, what do you want to be?" I'd wait for the question because it was an easy one for me. I was very clear. "I am going to be a writer." I knew this with absolute certainty because that's what I was, even then. I would plot

1

and dream and fill scribbler after scribbler with stories, mostly tragic, about heroic dogs, cowgirls, princesses and gypsies. I could not have imagined then that I would one day be writing about osso buco and marmalade and bird's nest soup. Only now, in retrospect, do I see the logic of it all.

Fresh lobster, summer's wild berries and fiddleheads in spring were staples of my Nova Scotia childhood. As were neon-green Jell-O salads and baked beans from a can. It all tasted good to me. I was first in line to lick the bowl when my Gran made boiled icing. And every year, because he knew me well, Santa would leave a jar of fat green pimento-stuffed olives in my Christmas stocking. It would be years before I discovered there was any other kind, by which time I was steadily refining my culinary repertoire in other ways as well.

I had mastered the three-bean salad. I made chili con carne, apple crisp, and festive dips with Lipton onion soup. But the best was yet to come. Through sheer good fortune, and none too soon, I married a man who, to my great amazement, had never in his entire life eaten a Big Mac or microwaved popcorn or smeared Cheez Whiz on celery sticks. Needless to say, I was fascinated. And so, it seems, was he: here was a woman who'd not tasted risotto or eaten an artichoke that hadn't come from a jar. Doors opened for both of us, some more promising than others. I soon kicked my Hamburger Helper habit and, over time, came to discover the joys of preparing and sharing real food. The logical next step was to put this journey of discovery into words.

What follows is a collection of ruminations and remembrances assembled over an eight-year association with the

Times Colonist in Victoria, B.C. I am grateful to my editor there, Carolyn Heiman, for creating this opportunity for me. I am also indebted to former New Yorker, seasoned editor and friend Robert Amussen. His enthusiasm and skilled guidance helped shape and polish a chaotic and sprawling manuscript. Most of all, I thank my husband, Chris Bayliss, for opening my eyes, holding my hand, and sharing, with such a generous heart, his love of food and fun.

Pie in the Sky

I wish that I'd wake up one day to find the whole world
coated in chocolate.

I wish that lobsters bred like rabbits and oysters grew
on trees.

I wish all eggs had double yolks and lambs were
millepedes.

I wish cholesterol didn't count.

I wish that the butter could find its way to the
bottom of the popcorn bag. (A refinement
that depends, of course, on the preceding
wish being granted.)

I wish Miss Vickie lived next door.
Paul Newman too, come to think of it.

I wish I had a stand-in to eat my Brussels
sprouts.

I wish the wines I can afford tasted like
the wines I like to drink.

I wish that farmers were as
highly valued as baseball players.

I wish truffles were a dime a dozen
and zucchini was impossible to grow.

I wish there really was pie in the sky.

1

Open Wide

*The primary requisite
to writing well about food
is a good appetite.*

A. J. LIEBLING

Breakfast with Grandad

It all began where life itself begins, with an egg. And a man who taught me reverence for this simplest and most perfect of foods.

Grandad ate two boiled eggs for breakfast every morning. He would slide the eggs into gently boiling water, set out a plate, a knife, a small spoon and a double eggcup. On the side of the plate he put a nub of butter and a small mound of salt. Then he'd put the kettle on for tea. At some critical point, usually after the salt and before the kettle whistled, he put a slice of bread into the toaster. When the toast popped up the eggs were done.

I loved to watch my grandad cooking eggs. There was an elegance to this homely, unhurried routine. Perhaps because he was so very tall and, in my eyes, so very handsome, or perhaps it was because he always wore a jacket and tie even to the breakfast table, but it seemed to me that the presentation of eggs took on all the gravity and refinement of a great occasion.

Perhaps too—I can't be sure—I'd heard the stories of Grandad on the road. He had come to Canada with an English soccer team and decided that while he was in the neighbourhood he might as well take a look around. Which he did, on foot, following the railway lines from Montreal to Vancouver, where his eight-month journey ended in the fall of 1906. His diary records the details of this extraordinary trek: the prairie landscape, the mountains, the people he met, and the meals he managed to scrounge along the way. Mostly, he ate eggs—stolen from a henhouse after dark, shared with a friendly stationmaster, "fried to a turn, six of them, for supper."

Often, on a Sunday morning, he would cook eggs for the two of us, always boiled, always in double eggcups. I'd watch as he picked up his knife and, with exquisite aim and understatement, sliced off the top of his egg. Anxiously, I would attempt the same manouevre, shards of shell exploding in every direction like a small grenade. I would press a button of butter into the egg's warm centre, dip spoon into salt and then into the hot bright yolk. Sometimes I'd dunk my toast, but only when he wasn't looking because he frowned on this. One didn't dunk toast. Nor did one rain salt all over one's food. Or butter one's toast all in one go. I wanted very much to please him, so I never did.

Boiled eggs are still my favourite way to start the day. I don't own a double eggcup, though I've searched high and low for one. I use an egg timer now because our thrift-shop toaster refuses to acknowledge the three-minute rule. And I dunk my toast, which is buttered all over, because I'm grown up now and can do as I please.

But these refinements have in no way diminished the sense of occasion and the sweet, insistent tug of my past that accompanies the ceremonial boiling and serving of eggs.

I consider the egg to be the perfect food, perfectly packaged and chock-full of all things necessary to life. I eat eggs because they comfort and nourish. And because they take me back and take me home—for breakfasts on Sundays with Grandad.

Other memories are shaped by the sea and childhood summers spent at a tiny cottage on Nova Scotia's north shore. The salt air—saltier by far, it seems to me, than our West Coast facsimile—smelled sharp and clean, and its touch was cool even on the hottest days. I remember the scrape of sand in the bedclothes and our terrifying encounters with jellyfish, some as big as dinner plates with stingers four feet long. And, at our doorstep, a feast of good food: lobster, which couldn't have cost much more than a hot dog does today, was a summertime staple. Crabs too, huge ones, though we were far too skittish to catch them ourselves. And snails.

We didn't call them snails, of course. I don't suppose we'd have eaten them if anyone had bothered to point out that that was what they were. We knew them as periwinkles. And as kids we'd spend entire days scrambling among the rocks, slip-sliding on carpets of seaweed in our bare feet, gathering periwinkles for the evening's meal.

The ritual eating of periwinkles (steamed first, of course—the adults took care of that end of things) was both gruesome and thrilling and, I suspect, far more satisfying than the periwinkle itself. The idea of eating one's supper with a pin held immense appeal. You'd first flick off the little black cap that guards the entrance to the tiny creature's shell. Then you'd spear the snail itself, dip it into a puddle of butter, and down it would slide, each minuscule morsel an exotic, precious prize.

Behind our little cottage were a water pump, an outhouse and Farmer Fraser's fields. That's what we called him, Farmer Fraser. He grew hay for the most part, but from time to time, in the acreage bordering our makeshift badminton court, Farmer Fraser planted corn.

They say a farmer can sit in his field at night and actually listen to the corn grow, hear the sigh of the stretching stalk, the whisper of leaves unfurling. I imagined I could hear it too and I'd wait, as if for Christmas, for the day when Mr. Fraser stopped by to say the corn was ready.

The night of the corn boil heralded the last lap of a long, sweet summer, a night when joy jostled uneasily with thoughts of back-to-school haircuts, starched blouses and the weighty prospect of wearing shoes again. We'd build a bonfire on the beach, roll the cooked corn in bricks of butter and eat marshmallows, speared on a stick and burned to a crisp.

These memories are as deep and strong as the pull of the sea. Which is why, every once in a while, the Maritimer in me stirs herself, whimpers soulfully, and begs to go home. But it's a long way. And it's been a long time. So I head for the kitchen instead. You can always find your way home through the kitchen.

Food is memory-rich territory, loaded with sensual reminders that stay with us all our lives. The smell of gingerbread still transports me to my grandmother's kitchen in Pictou, Nova Scotia. The house was big and creaky and the rooms very cold, except for the kitchen, which bloomed with heat from Granny's coal-fired stove. She would make her gingerbread in a big square pan and portion it out while it was still warm—no thought of waiting till dessert. We would sit at the kitchen table with the blue oilcloth cover and wait for our share of the thick yellow cream that she'd spoon off the milk from the bottle. But what I remember most fondly about Granny's gingerbread are the raisins— sweet and plentiful, swollen from the heat.

My mother used to make apple pies, an event that stands out in my memory because she so rarely baked anything at all. She found cooking a chore. It bored her. But apple pie was like a siren's call and she'd bake all day, turning out pie after pie until the whole enterprise suddenly palled and we wouldn't see another pie for months. We'd have it warm with a slice of sharp cheddar, and that is how I prefer it still.

And then there was toad-in-the-hole, my father's specialty and, quite possibly, his own invention. It bore no resemblance to the English original, a breakfast sausage tucked into a nest of dumpling dough. In our house toad-in-the-hole was white bread with a hole cut in the middle to accommodate an egg. The whole lot was then fried up in a splatter of bacon fat and served with ketchup.

No one growing up in Nova Scotia can leave childhood behind without a fond look back at the blueberry patch. The gathering of blueberries is associated with sunlit days, salt air, a dozen cousins and a Scottie dog named Tizzy. Armed with kitchen pots and sand pails, we'd forage for hours, one eye ever alert for poison ivy, the other cast balefully on a cousin's pail, which, it seemed to me, filled up so much faster than my own. Then it was back home for the treat to beat all summer treats: blueberry grunt. (Oh yes, the name would set us off every time, spluttering and tittering behind our hands at the naughtiness of it all.) Blueberry grunt is an old Nova Scotia dish sometimes referred to as "fungy" or "slump," a combination of stewed fruit—strawberries perhaps, rhubarb maybe, but blueberries were definitely best—with dumplings heaped on top.

Blueberry Grunt

This is the real thing, a favourite Maritime summer classic, from Marie Nightingale's wonderful collection, Out of Old Nova Scotia Kitchens. *She doesn't say how many this will serve. She does, however, mention that it often constituted an entire meal. You decide. My hunch is that four small, very hungry children would be only too happy to call this dinner and have done with it. Grown-ups might prefer to apportion it six ways and call it dessert.*

1 quart blueberries
½ cup sugar (or more)
½ cup water

Put berries, sugar and water in a pot, cover and boil gently until there is plenty of juice (about 5 minutes).

Dumplings
2 cups flour
4 teaspoons baking powder
½ teaspoon salt
1 teaspoon sugar

1 tablespoon butter
1 tablespoon shortening
¼ to ½ cup milk

Sift the flour, baking powder, salt and sugar into a bowl. Cut in the butter and shortening and add enough milk to make a soft biscuit dough. Drop by spoonfuls onto the hot blueberries. Cover closely and do not peek for 15 minutes. Serve hot.

Intimations in a Porridge Pot

In my junior high-school days I had a teacher called Miss Johnson. She was a glum-faced woman who taught what we then called Domestic Science, which is where the girls were herded while the boys were in Shop making ashtrays for their dads. Porridge is what I remember most vividly from her class. I never did get the hang of porridge—it was full of lumps and stuck to the pot—and I was summarily dispatched to the sewing circle to make aprons instead.

Little wonder, then, that at the tender age of five, seeking perhaps to compensate for the glaring culinary cracks in his small domestic world, my middle son asked for an Easy-Bake oven for Christmas. He quickly graduated from thimble-size cupcakes to kitchen artistry on a grander scale. While his brothers were building Dagwood-style sandwich towers from Kraft spreads and bologna, he would fashion his own more refined version, intricately assembled and cut into trim triangles with the crusts fastidiously removed. Today he is a trained and accomplished chef.

Obviously, this talented young man did not inherit his culinary skills from me. Or his dad. Family meals in those days were unremarkable by any standard: meat loaf, mash, frozen peas and maybe, on a special day, a Sara Lee cake with ice cream. He'd not have found me twittering about in the kitchen coaxing along a béchamel sauce or bathing small birds in raspberry coulis. My appetite for food did not translate readily into the sure-handed intimacy that comes so effortlessly to the intuitive cook. It was years before I discovered that tournedos were not a weather phenomenon and that you could actually put together a meal without a can of mushroom soup.

No, if there is such a thing as a cookery gene it's definitely a recessive one. It bypassed me. If it graced my mother she either failed to notice or shooed it away. But it was in full flower for sure in my granny, whose rice pudding and raisin pies feed my memories still.

I've decided, based on nothing even remotely scientific, that the craft of cookery is a unique confluence of many blessings. When my son cooks, I watch. I watch his hands, the easy touch that coaxes flour and butter into pastry; the brisk *chunk-chunk* of the knife that reduces a handful of garlic into a dice as fine as confetti; when he leans over the soup pot I lean too—something with lentils, smelling marvellous. He dips a finger and tastes. I dip too, and taste. He's not sure.

"Salt?" I venture.

No. Not salt.

He slices a lemon, squeezes its juice into the bubbling pot and tastes again.

There. The soup is ready. It's good, so good.

There's more at work here, I decide, than merely knowing how. Know-how comes from experience, from learning as you go. It's know-how that informs you how salt reacts with yeast. And how to test the doneness of steak with the prod of a thumb. But what separates a practiced cook from an inspired one is a different ingredient entirely, something as deeply rooted and mysterious as a bird's sense of the stars. It's *knowing*. And like dancing, some get it, some don't. You may master all the moves but if you don't feel the music you'll never know the joy.

And then there's passion. By this I mean not merely a passion for food that, untempered, translates simply and clumsily into gluttony. The brilliant cook consumes *life*. He's as enchanted by the arching light of a rainbow as he is by a well-plumped omelet. His passion springs from a generous heart. There's no room at the stove for the mean-spirited whose food will never seduce because they have nothing of themselves to give. Their kitchens, you can be sure, are as neat as a pin, but their soups are thin, their muffins mingy, and they always, always skimp on the chocolate chips.

When she was young, my aunt Nan earned herself a loyal following with her magnanimous ways with all things all kids love best: chocolate cake with boiled icing, strawberries and cream, cinnamon-sprinkled toast. But her signature treat was her egg salad sandwiches. They were thick and squishy and demanded a careful grip by two small hands to heft from plate to mouth. The bread was soft. Tiny chunks of gherkin and celery lent a satisfying crunch to each mouthful. And Aunt Nan would monitor our pleasure, asking, "Are they good? Eat up. There's more, you know, where that came from."

"Cooking is like love—it should be entered into with abandon, or not at all." This observation was made in 1956 by Harriet Van Horne in *Vogue* magazine. And borne out by a loving aunt and a gifted son, whose secret—I know this now—is a bigness of heart, and happiness freely shared.

A Very Comforting Lentil Soup

In theory, this recipe serves six. In our house it serves one: me. I'm the soup lover in the family. I am also, by default, the soup maker, and this simple, robust potful has seen me through many long, soggy winter days.

¼ cup olive oil
¾ cup diced onion
½ cup diced celery
½ cup diced carrot
3 cloves garlic, minced
Salt and pepper
½ teaspoon dried thyme
1 sprig fresh rosemary
⅓ cup dry white wine
½ cup good-quality canned tomatoes, cut up, with their juice
½ cup lentils (French Puy are the tastiest by far and are less likely to turn to mush in the cooking)

6 cups chicken stock (homemade is best but low-salt
 canned broth is fine too)
1 tablespoon fresh-squeezed lemon juice

Heat the oil in a heavy saucepan over medium heat. Add the onion, celery, carrots and garlic and cook gently, stirring from time to time, until they are softened (about 20 minutes). Add a pinch of salt, some freshly ground pepper, the thyme and rosemary. Stir and continue to cook the mixture over medium heat for another 2 to 3 minutes. Add the wine, stir, and let this bubble away until the liquid is reduced (about 5 minutes).

Stir in the tomatoes, lentils and stock and let the soup simmer lazily, partially covered, until the lentils are tender (about 40 minutes). Stir in the lemon juice, check for seasoning and serve.

Serves 6.

Words Fail Me

No, I've decided, is one of those words that's impossible to say with your mouth full. *No* means no pizza for me, thanks. No gravy. No ice cream. No seconds. *No* means that whatever's on offer I'm not getting any. I have trouble with that. I like to leave myself a little wiggle room.

The truth is, my tummy has a mind of its own. It can be a

regular little hellion at times. It is very partial to peanut butter, for example. And Skor bars. But what it really loves is chicken skin, when we sneak up on the roasted bird while it's still in the pan and scrape the little nuggets of crispy cholesterol right out of the warm fat. My tummy loves that.

To be honest, I have a certain amount of sympathy for the demands my tummy puts on me. It works hard and rarely complains about what comes its way. It accepts, without a hiccup, wholesome grains and salad greens, beet tops, even garbanzo beans. So I'm not surprised when, every once in a while, it figures enough is enough and heads like a heat-seeking missile for the Jelly Bellys.

No is one of those words I've relegated to my back-pocket vocabulary. Like *mellifluous*. And *inchoate*. It's there should I ever feel the occasion warrants. Needless to say, many such occasions have presented themselves over the years. Pizza's the usual culprit. I am inordinately fond of pizza and have been since that landmark day, some thirty years ago, when I met the pizza of my dreams at George's Spaghetti House in Toronto.

George's was housed in a seedy-looking building in the wrong part of town. Some of the city's best jazz musicians played here on weekend evenings. The music was cool. The wine was cheap. And the pizza—mushrooms and pepperoni and thick, chewy cheese—was divine.

I was hooked. At first, my habit—for that is certainly what it was—amounted to no more than one pizza fix per weekend, an indulgence that seemed to me both manageable and easily rationalized. Pizza, I told myself, was God's way of delivering all four food groups in one thoughtfully balanced, perfectly assembled package.

Then my job relocated me to an office within walking distance of my source. This was like letting someone with a shoe fetish run amok in a Bata warehouse. And George's, wouldn't you know it, was open for lunch. With my habit now threatening to become a Monday-to-Friday affair, I knew I needed help. Instead, I found a soul mate. Judith, a fellow junkie, was always pathetically willing to answer the call whenever lunchtime rolled around. Off we'd toddle, two pizza-crazies, two and three times a week. We hit rock bottom together. What saved me in the end was not iron resolve but good fortune. I met the man I was to marry. And I changed jobs.

The man's name is Chris. He is witty and elegant, an English gentleman. I fell in love, instantly, over lunch: tarte aux asperges at the oh-so-smart Le Trou Normande in Toronto's Yorkville district. I'd suggested George's. He'd demurred. The thing is, you see—and he broke this to me gently—he did not eat pizza. (It's the gooey cheese. He swears he was frightened by a fondue when he was a child.) This was a blow, of course, as he seemed quite perfect in every other respect. But there were compensations. It was Chris who weaned me off Hamburger Helper and introduced me to seviche, Peking duck, baclava, brandy-dipped, sugared strawberries, tiramisu and the wild, macho-fish taste of fresh mackerel from a Portuguese fishmonger in Kensington Market.

He has four children. I, a widow when we met, have three.

Together we had seven mouths to feed, a brand-new bigger-than-both-of-us mortgage and someone else's habits of a lifetime to tiptoe around. It was an exciting, sometimes daunting, and altogether delicious new world.

It was also somewhat disorienting. My pizza fixes were becoming more and more sporadic, and my affair with George was rapidly losing steam. But my new job was the clincher. It delivered me uptown, to trendier environs and a whole new restaurant culture: the rarified and minimalist world of nouvelle cuisine. Pizza now came ultra-thin and dressed to the nines with feta cheese, baby shrimp and arugula. Cute pizza drives me crazy. I went cold turkey without missing a beat.

I make my own pizza now—not often, mind you, as it's a solo indulgence still—but when I do I invoke my old mentor, George, and do it his way. It's a labour of love. It's my gift to me. Why would I say *no?*

The word becomes a particularly elusive one when we're travelling. During a visit to England a few years ago Chris and I treated ourselves to a slap-up meal at Rules, in London. This was quintessential British fare, hearty to a fault, and wheeled to our table under domes of gleaming silver: roast beef (its pink bulk barely contained by the platter in front of me), mash, the obligatory two veg, a tsunami of gravy and, defying the critical mass that had by now accumulated, Yorkshire pudding. Then, what to our wondering eyes should appear? More pudding: sweet this time, and heavy as a brick, for afters.

We might have managed tolerably well if we weren't off to the theatre immediately afterward. We'd chosen a play by

Michael Frayne, *Noises Off*. It was uproariously funny. Side-splitting, double-up funny. Except we couldn't double up. We were too full. Everyone around us was doubling up but all we could do was hold on tight and ride out the pain.

Nevertheless, following quickly on the heels of the Rules incident came the Olde English Tea Shoppe marathon, which should have been nipped in the bud with a firm *no* right from the get-go. We'd left London and were touring the countryside, which is where I met my first cream tea. And a wondrous thing it was! A bracing brew of good, strong tea accompanied by warm scones, lavishly buttered, heaped with strawberry jam and topped with a silky cumulus of clotted cream.

I was smitten. My tummy was thrilled to bits. And that was that, I'm afraid. Our fate was sealed. The rest of our itinerary was predicated upon the promise of scones and jam and clotted cream at the end of the road. The "n" word did not cross my mind, or my lips, even once. And rarely since.

2

From Where I Sit

It's not what you serve that matters most,
it's who you choose to share it.

ANONYMOUS

Guess Who's Coming for Breakfast?

There was a time when I was paid large sums of money to persuade people to buy all manner of things they didn't know they needed: chocolate bars, TV dinners, hamburgers, dog biscuits and dishwasher detergent with special cleaning action that promised "virtually spotless" results every time. I thrived in this fantasy land called advertising, whose inhabitants truly believed that good things came in microwavable packages and where grown-up people spent the better part of a day tweezing sesame seeds on a burger bun until it was camera-perfect. No matter. I worked hard and, for a while, I lived like a queen. Life was a banquet. And I lapped it up.

Then, one day, a most extraordinary thing happened. I stepped back from my laden table and decided I'd had my fill. I yearned for less, not more.

That was August 1989. August in Toronto is brutal. The air curdles in the heat, leaving you limp and breathless. That particular summer we managed to escape, to holiday on the islands off the British Columbia coast. Which is how, one golden afternoon, I came to find myself on a white shell beach with the sun on my face announcing that this was where I wanted to live. My husband, equally dream-struck, agreed that this was a fine idea. It was also a doable one: our brood had fledged. Our nest was empty.

A very wise friend of mine once offered up this advice: *Make decisions with your heart,* he said, *and look after the details with your head.*

So we did. We followed our hearts to Galiano, a tiny jewel of an island thousands of miles from the city I'd called home for twenty-five years.

It took a year to work out the details, not the least of which was the fallout from the deep-discount sale of our Toronto house during the most spectacular real estate slump in decades. Nonetheless, we headed west—with a financial cushion significantly less cushiony than we had bargained for. Just one prickly detail remained unresolved: how to make up for the shortfall.

There wasn't a huge demand on this island of nine-hundred-odd self-sufficient souls for our rather specialized skills: corporate communications (Chris's stock in trade) or catchy jingles (mine). In the dozen or more years we've lived here not a single potter, painter, fisherman or farmer has commissioned me to write a jingle. Or found themselves stuck for a shareholder's report at the end of the fiscal year.

We weighed our options. Fishing was out: we didn't know how and there weren't enough fish to go around anyway. Neither of us is particularly adept with a chainsaw. Or a bulldozer. There were opportunities in other fields—roofing, carpentry, blasting, tree surgery, chimney cleaning and well drilling—but we didn't qualify. So we opened a bed-and-breakfast.

This, of course, involved food, a mutual passion. And the art of hospitable chit-chat, which we figured we'd get the hang of eventually. Kitchen duties came easily. The role of cheery greeter fell to the host who could muster the jolliest smile at breakfast time. The tasks of bed stripper, dish-washer, tub scrubber and dust buster were fairly shared. And we were delighted and appalled, in equal measure, by the people who passed through our door.

There was the unhappy accountant from Texas. She worked for a savings and loan company at a time when sav-ings and loan companies were reeling from allegations of creative numbers-juggling and other fiscal hanky-panky. She wasn't sleeping well. Her stomach was acting up. She ate toast and tea and spent a lot of time in the tub. She didn't want to go home.

There was the couple who shared the egg: he ate the yolk, she ate the white. They washed the lot down with mugs of hot water and thanked us effusively for a very fine breakfast indeed.

We had the pleasure of the company of a bona fide Lord and Lady: he rolled up his trousers and paddled in the sea. She wrote an ode to fresh-baked bread and the sprawling cedar that pressed against the window where they slept.

There were people who arrived as strangers and left as friends—friends we still hold dear today. And then there were the Biggers.

The Biggers were as their name implies, Mr. being only marginally more so than Mrs. During the welcoming cere-monies, I did some quick calculations involving mass, weight and the approximate acreage of a king-size bed, and came up short. They were a cheerful twosome whose central preoccupation became obvious very quickly.

"Hi," said Mr. Bigger. "I'm Jack. This is my wife, Myrna. And this I gather is your breakfast menu." It was. And they fell upon it hungrily.

The menu was a generous one: fresh-squeezed orange juice, a bowl of fruit, a basket of fresh bread and muffins, assorted jams and marmalades. Additional offerings were available as well: eggs cooked to order in any way that took their fancy; bacon; homemade sage-and-leek pork sausages; granola; waffles with maple syrup or fruit; and kippers. The kippers were red herrings, really. Nobody seriously entertained the notion of starting a day with kippers.

We asked the Biggers to mark their selections on the menu and leave it with us before they tucked in for the night. This they did. But they'd obviously misunderstood. They'd checked off everything. Everything except kippers. Some things, like sausages, had been checked off four times. They'd asked for an omelet. They'd also requested boiled eggs. Twice. And waffles.

I pasted on my hostess smile and approached them that evening.

"I just want to make sure I have this right," I said brightly. "We don't want any surprises in the morning!"

We went over the menu once again.

"Sausages?" I queried. "Is that sausages for one? Or two?"

"That's a double order of sausages. Each."

"Ah." My smile widened. "These aren't your average

sausages. You should know that." My hands described the length and breadth of our sausage largesse.

They nodded.

"And bacon?"

"And bacon."

Of course.

"Now, the egg thing. You'll both have boiled eggs . . . ?"

"Two. We'll both have two."

"Wonderful!" I chirped. "So I'll scratch the omelet."

"I'll have the omelet," said Mr. Bigger. He was looking at me oddly, concentrating in the manner of someone trying to make sense of a foreign language. "I'll have the omelet. After the boiled eggs."

"Ah."

"And," he added, "we'll have the waffles after the eggs." Myrna was nodding. Yes, she too would have waffles. After the eggs.

"With syrup?"

They considered.

"Fruit," said Myrna. "With a little syrup on the side." Mr. Bigger seemed pleased with that arrangement.

"Right!" I said. "And no kippers."

They looked at me as if I were some sort of simpleton. "No kippers."

We got up early. There was much to do.

The Biggers chose to have breakfast on the deck, which allowed us, from our vantage point at the stove, to observe their progress and choreograph our kitchen calisthenics accordingly. The granola was produced along with the coffee and the fruit and the muffins and the bread. When the bread basket was emptied I stuffed it full again. I boiled eggs and rolled sausages around on the griddle while Chris fried bacon and waited for my signal to begin the intricate shake-slide-toss routine with the omelet pan.

The waffle iron was pressed into action, jam pots were replenished and syrup dispensed. Back and forth we trotted with laden trays and happy chatter to the tune of the stove timer's ping.

They ate gravely and methodically, heaving themselves to their feet from time to time to limber up for the next course. I thought of the man who exploded at the table in the Monty Python film *The Meaning of Life*. My mind cantered back two thousand years to the mealtime marathons of the Romans: jellyfish and sea urchins and flamingo tongues and stuffed sows' udders, followed by boiled ostrich, turtledoves, parrots, ham and whole roasted fallow deer with onion sauce. Then, after a snooze or a leisurely tub, the plucky diner would hitch up his toga and turn his attention to a groaning board of pastries and cakes and honey-fried nuts.

At this point, and just in the nick of time, an alert slave with his trusty throat tickler would leap into action, exhort the diner to "open wide" and off to the vomitorium he'd go. I felt a stab of alarm at having failed to provide such amenities for our guests.

They lingered over coffee, burping dreamily, and left soon afterwards, their pockets bulging with muffins. We subsequently cancelled the all-you-can-eat breakfast concept and went continental.

The Bigger-the-Better Muffin

The Biggers, as noted, loved these exceptionally hearty, all-you-can-eat-at-one-go muffins.

2 cups all-purpose flour
1 cup sugar
2 teaspoons baking soda
1 teaspoon cinnamon
½ teaspoon salt
1 cup grated carrot
½ cup raisins
½ cup chopped nuts
1 apple, peeled, cored and grated
1 teaspoon grated orange zest
3 eggs
1 cup salad oil
1 teaspoon vanilla

Preheat oven to 350°F. Grease a muffin pan.

In a large bowl, combine flour, sugar, baking soda, cinnamon and salt. Stir in carrot, raisins, nuts, apple and zest. In a smaller bowl beat together the eggs, oil and vanilla. Lightly fold the egg mixture into the dry ingredients until just combined.

Spoon into muffin cups, filling each one to the top.

Bake for 30 minutes or until a toothpick inserted in the centre of a muffin comes out dry. Cool in pan before removing.

Makes 12 muffins.

I'll Take Potluck

Four years and 187 breakfasts after the Biggers' visit, we ushered out the last of our paying guests and reclaimed our precious mornings for ourselves. Our financial cushion was as tatty and deflated as it had ever been. But we didn't care. We'd dished up all the waffles and sausages and cheerful "good mornings" we could muster. Our smiles were wearing thin. Island life, the idyll that had seduced us in the first place, was passing us by. It was time to feed ourselves.

On Galiano, a meal shared with friends is a taste of life at its richest, most satisfying best.

Come! Come for dinner, the neighbours say. *There'll be eight of us, or maybe ten. Could you bring a dessert? And a bottle of wine?*

Of course! Whatever. And, with a little help from your friends, dinner's on and the evening unfolds. You arrive with a dog at your heels and your apple pie, still warm in its pan, to join the crush in the kitchen. Too many cooks? No such thing. And there's barely room on the table for all that's on offer: home-smoked salmon, loaves of dimpled, garlic-studded focaccia, lasagna, green salads, roasted peppers—red, yellow, orange, green—bathed in oil and balsamic vinegar. There are pakoras and grilled chorizos and corn chips and a fiery green salsa. The beer is cold, the wine is young and tastes of blackberries, and there's little danger of running out of either. That this hodgepodge of textures and tastes defies all laws of culinary propriety bothers no one. Hodgepodge is good, infinitely preferable to the meal hijacked by a dozen bean salads and a cheese log.

Potluck means no guarantees. You take what comes. And I love it.

In my other life, my helter-skelter city life, having people for dinner was cause for both celebration and nervous collapse. We didn't attempt it often. The days were too short: there were far too few pockets of hard-earned time between endless work and endless errands and the needs of our various children. Nevertheless, from time to time we'd hurl ourselves into the fray, fly about the kitchen like things possessed and slump, exhausted, at evening's end swearing we'd never do *that* again.

You could always buy your way out of this angst, of course. There was a gourmet take-out, the perfect cop-out, on every corner. Instant hospitality for the rich and the weary. There was no stigma attached to this indulgence either. Quite the contrary. That La-di-Da Catering tray in your curbside trash said as much about you and your privileged lifestyle as the Porsche in your three-car garage.

We didn't have a Porsche. We had a Honda Civic. And no garage. So gourmet-to-go was never an option as far as we were concerned. Besides, it galled me to pay $10 for a chicken breast tarted up with olives and prunes when I could toss the same thing together in my own kitchen for a fraction of the price. It seemed to me that an invitation to dinner was a rather hollow gesture if you couldn't spare a little of yourself in the process. All of which is fine and dandy, of course, if there's any leftover self to spare. Which, in my experience, there rarely was.

The concept of "potluck" was unheard of amongst the city dwellers we knew. You wouldn't dream of inviting friends to a meal and asking them to please bring the food. *Poor things*, they'd say. *They've lost their grip for sure.* Happily, bring-and-share is standard fare here on the island I now call home. Birthdays, Saturday-night get-togethers, even weddings are often cobbled-together affairs with guests turning up to witness the vows with bowls of tabouleh and warm bread and armloads of flowers.

A potluck meal is like a barn raising. It brings us together in common purpose. It asks that each of us do our part and contribute what we can. But, sadly, shared experiences like these are simply not part of the fabric of most of our lives. This is a pity, because the potluck ritual enriches our times together in ways beyond the time and money saved. It says a lot about the lives we choose to live.

Someone once said that if we are to survive as a culture we must rediscover the social skein of village life. We must reinvent that place where neighbour reaches out to neighbour, where the old and the young, the needy and the able not merely coexist but contribute to the shared dynamic that benefits us all. The potluck meal, like an old-fashioned barn raising, offers us a place of honour among friends. And—along with the potato salads that just keep coming—a taste of the very best of village life.

Sue's Famous Potluck Sticky Chicken
Sue—friend, creative cook and long-time Islander—calls this "free-wheeling" potluck fare: easy-going and infinitely adaptable.

No ketchup in the house? Use salsa instead. Or ready-made tomato sauce. Want to kick up the heat? Add chili flakes. Chicken skin off or chicken skin on? Your choice. And remember, there's no such thing as too much garlic.

12 to 16 chicken thighs
6 cloves garlic, crushed
½ cup ketchup
¼ cup molasses
¼ cup soy sauce
2 tablespoons apple cider vinegar
2 tablespoons lemon juice
2 tablespoons honey

Preheat oven to 325°F.

Place the chicken thighs in a well-greased roasting pan. (Sue uses Pam. Pam uses vegetable oil.) Combine the remaining ingredients and pour the mixture over the chicken. Cover the pan. If it doesn't have a lid you can use foil, just make sure it's tightly wrapped.

Bake for about 1 hour, shaking the pan vigorously every 15 minutes or so to make sure the chicken is well coated and not sticking. (Add a few drops of water to the pan if the chicken begins to stick.) The chicken's done when the meat is barely clinging to the bones. Serve it up as finger food at room temperature, with plenty of Wet-Wipes.

Makes 12 to 16 thighs

My Life as a Hunter-gatherer

The truly miraculous aspect of country living was one I'd not anticipated. I discovered food. Honest-to-goodness food, clotted-with-the-earth-it-grew-in food. No shrink wrap, no pre-wash, no dressing-included.

We had abandoned our city lives with only vaguely formed notions of what the trade-offs would be. The exchange rate was pretty much fixed in some respects. We'd have a whole lot less money. And a great deal more time: great, luxurious, uncomplicated stretches of time to study the stars, make bread, walk in the woods and read, finally, the thousand and one books we'd carted with us from one end of the country to the other.

What I'd not counted on was my accidental life as a hunter-gatherer.

I'd had some experience with the mystery and magic of found food. Those long-ago Nova Scotia summers by the sea introduced me to the delights of banqueting on periwinkles and blueberries. Afloat on inner tubes, we could watch, through sun-spangled water, as our lobster supper inched its way toward the trap that would ensnare it. And the delights of early mornings, bare feet in damp grass, and mushrooms.

Mushrooms grew in the field where the bull hung out, his presence a guarantee, so I was told, of plentiful pickings. We would head out in the first pink light of day, my aunt Nan and I. Why, of all the grown-ups and armies of children who shared our summer space, we were always the first to greet the day, I'll never know. But off we'd go, plotting a cautious course around the dreaded bull who was never far away.

Aunt Nan brought to the hunt nothing but the housecoat she wore. She'd hold it up at the hem and I'd deposit the mushrooms in its fold. They were, I realize now, *Agaricus campestris*, the common meadow mushroom. And what mushrooms they were! Some as big as saucers but mostly fat, pale buttons with pink gills and so thick on the ground that we would invariably decide to leave a housecoat load for another day.

Then, before anyone else was awake, we'd have them sizzling in butter and piled on toast for our breakfast by the window above the sea. Between us, we'd polish off the lot, having agreed, I suppose, that if anyone else wanted mushrooms for breakfast they could jolly well stir their stumps and get their own.

Memories of those mornings come back with a sweet rush when I prowl the woods today. Our forests are full of delectables. In late October, early November, the chanterelles appear. By December, when the earth is soggy with the winter's rain, I may be lucky enough to find a pine mushroom or two, the coveted *Armillaria ponderosa*. This magnificent specimen tastes like a wood-smoked steak and sits in your hand as heavy as a melon. Often, in the spring, in a charmed spot in the woods nearby, I will find morels: two, maybe three, never more, and all the more precious for being so elusive. I know a place where a mossy log produces oyster mushrooms by the handful. And shaggy manes appear, as if by magic, in our driveway like gifts left in the night. Such bounty! Discovered quite by accident, as the seasons unfolded and I found my way around.

Most people are aghast at the notion of gathering mushrooms, convinced I am flirting with instant death. This is a mind-set I encourage, quite frankly. I figure that fear of foraging is Nature's way of containing demand and ensuring plentiful pickings for me. Besides, I use a guidebook and follow two simple rules: if in doubt, throw it out. Or delegate any experimental tastings to someone outside the immediate family.

The truth is that mushroom gathering is not for everyone. The guileless and the generous hearted, for example, do very poorly in the field. They tend to be blurters, determined, in their innocence, to share their good fortune with all and sundry.

This is behaviour quite unbecoming the seasoned 'shroomer, who, in this neck of the woods anyway, will go to almost any lengths to keep his patch a secret. So if you want to play the game and stake your claim you have to know the rules.

First of all, there is a dress code: what you wear must in no way reveal what you're up to. Surveyors' equipment, for instance, will take you almost anywhere without your true mission being uncovered. If you're in the woods, you could carry a chainsaw. In an open field, a butterfly net. Or a picnic basket. Whatever it takes to throw your fellow forager off the scent.

My preferred disguise is bird-watcher gear, the essential feature of which is a jacket, roomy and multi-pocketed. The pockets must be deep enough to conceal a good supply of paper bags (for your harvest), a couple of field guides (birds, for diversionary purposes; mushrooms, so you know what you're picking) and binoculars. You're here for the junco count. You wouldn't know a toadstool from a truffle if your life depended on it. Remember this.

Stealth is everything. You must learn to skulk. It takes a highly skilled skulker to slip into shadows and behind trees at a moment's notice. Also, you must learn the art of manipulating the truth while fixing your interrogator with a firm, unwavering eye.

For instance, when caught in the act and asked if those little orange trumpet-shaped thingies in your brown paper bag might in fact be chanterelles, the following patter is recommended:

"Chanterelles?" Open your bag. Look amazed. *"Chanterelles*, you say? Well, I'll be! Is that what they are?"

At this juncture a dubious *tsk-tsk* is in order as you ponder aloud the possibility that they could in fact be the deadly *Chanterellus imposteratus* and you, for one, have no intention of putting your life on the line to find out.

So far so good. When asked where you spotted them, say, "Back there. By the mossy stump." (Mossy stumps are a dime a dozen in mushroom territory.)

While your inquisitor is thrashing about in the undergrowth "back there," you're home free with your booty sizzling smartly in the frying pan.

It's a distasteful bit of business, I know. However, if you're smart—or just plain foolhardy, depending on your point of

41

view—all this stealth and subterfuge becomes quite unnecessary. The trick is grit, greed, and weather conditions so inhospitable you are guaranteed unlimited, uninterrupted access to any mushroom patch within slogging distance.

My friend and I had planned just such a preemptive strike one grim, grey day in late October. I called her about noon, as the rain hammered on the windows, to cancel. A prudent decision from where I stood—warm and dry on the inside looking out. My friend wasn't so sure. She's tougher than I, a twenty-five-year veteran of this challenging climate.

It was a game of chicken. *I don't mind . . . a little rain doesn't bother me . . . well, it's up to you . . .* Who'd be the wimp to pull the plug on our plans—a jolly slosh through the forest in a downpour? Not me. So out I went in all my various leak-proof layers.

In the forest mosses glowed, as if lit from within, in various shades of green. Small rivers bubbled across our path. Our dogs danced through puddles, tongues lolling, their coats bright from the rain-wash. And everywhere you looked there were mushrooms. Honey-brown *Boletes. Russula,* wine-red and as big as your fist, shone through the clots of leaves underfoot. Tiny, furled fairy-fans (*Apricot Jelly*) lay in the path like discarded scraps of orange peel. *Navelcaps. Fairy Helmets.* Snow-white *Funnelcaps. Gypsy Nitecaps*—or were they *Autumn Skullcaps*? We leaned, heads together over our guidebook, puzzling over this one and that. The damp rose in our boots and slid off our chins.

But we were after chanterelles and there was only one spot they were likely to be. We had to leave the high ridge we were on and head downhill, where the path, almost obliterated now since the summer traffic had subsided, led to a valley trail. The rain fell more gently here, the forest canopy like a gauzy umbrella over our heads: chanterelle territory.

Almost at once I spotted one, a slice of pale orange thrusting up through the leaf-pack. And there were more, just off the trail where the salal grew thick, hip high and almost impenetrable, like hoops of barbed wire. We waded in.

In half an hour we'd filled a knapsack, and the dogs, having run their course, lay panting and dishevelled on the path. We were utterly drenched by now and we stood, grinning in the rain, awed at our great good fortune.

Jane Grigson, the English food writer, describes the chanterelle as "a curving trumpet with delicate ribs running from the stalk through to the under edge of the cap like fine vaulting." Its smell, according to some, resembles that of apricots. Ours didn't smell of apricots. Ours, waterlogged, smelled like wet earth, of rainforest in October. But we didn't care. We'd unearthed a treasure, that we knew, and nothing could dampen our spirits as we headed back through the dripping trees for home.

Chanterelles have a chewier consistency than the white supermarket mushrooms we're accustomed to and they should be coaxed along gently over low heat so they can cook at their leisure in their own juice. Which, once they'd been brushed clean, is what we did. With lots of butter, of course, and nothing more, because the deep-woodsy goodness of a fresh chanterelle needs no embellishment.

I'm convinced that nothing in the world tastes quite so good or nourishes more surely than this: found food, gathered and shared. There are echoes here of something yearned for but only vaguely recalled, discovered by chance, on paths too rarely travelled.

Chanterelles: Plain and Simple

One thing to remember: a chanterelle is not a zucchini. It is not tofu. It's not a frozen baby shrimp. It can stand on its own without cream sauces or Oriental spices or a coriander garnish despite a spate of elaborate recipes that would have you believe otherwise. In my opinion, all you need to make the most of a harvest of fresh chanterelles, or any wild mushrooms, is a mushroom brush, a frying pan and lots of butter.

The first thing to do is brush your mushrooms clean. Or wipe them, ever so gently, with a damp cloth. I never wash mushrooms. (They're probably rain-rinsed anyway and they should be absolutely dry before you cook them.) You can then slice them, lengthwise, if they're large. The little button-babies are fine as they are.

Next: butter. You are encouraged to throw caution to the wind here. Chanterelles *love* butter. Melt it in your pan over moderate heat until it starts to sizzle. Then add the mushrooms and stir them around till they're well drenched, lower the heat a bit, and let them cook, unrushed, until they're tender and their juices are released. You can scoop them from the pan and eat them now if you like. Or, if you can contain yourself for a minute or two (I can't), turn up the heat and give them a final toss-about, stir-fry style, until they're crispy at the edges and the juices are reduced.

They're marvellous either way. On toast, or not. With a little salt if that's your preference but I don't think they need it.

And there you have it: chanterelles, plain and simple. The best fast food on the planet.

Eat Your Greens

Fiddleheads speak to me of childhood and springtime. My mother would apportion them out as if they were the rarest of treasures—*one for you . . . one for me.* I'm not sure why I loved them so. I think I'd read somewhere that they'd been served to the queen on some royal visit or another, an endorsement that would have clinched it for sure.

I suspect there are people who've never clapped eyes on a fiddlehead, let alone tasted one. Or tromped in the rain through boot-sucking bogs to search them out. But if you (a) know what a fiddlehead is and (b) like to hunt and gather in places other than malls, it's hard to resist that once-a-year call of the wild, and the immense satisfaction that scavenging for lunch can bring.

If you know what you're looking for. And have the wits to resist when you don't. Which is why I'll probably pass on the fiddlehead hunt this year. I have memories enough from my last field trip to see me through many fiddlehead-free seasons to come.

I went on the hunt with the same faithful friend who shares my passion for chanterelles. We certainly looked like we knew what we were about with our field guides and mucky boots and our Little Red Riding Hood baskets. Unfortunately, we were a bit hazy on specifics. There's not a lot written about fiddleheads.

In his book *Stalking the Wild Asparagus,* Euell Gibbons makes no mention of fiddleheads amongst the many and varied wild edibles he gathers throughout the year. They appear nowhere in *Food,* that culinary gold mine assembled by Waverley Root. Incredibly, the Encyclopedia Britannica is silent on the subject as well. I eventually tracked them down in *The Oxford Companion to Food*; and they are given their due in the *Canadian Encyclopedia,* where they're identified as the leaf buds of the ostrich fern, *Matteuccia struthiopteris.*

Our field guide (*Plants of Coastal British Columbia* by Jim Pojar and Andy MacKinnon) directed us to the ostrich fern as well. It also posted a stern warning about another fern, bracken, which is carcinogenic and is known to have poisoned cattle grazing in the vicinity. I was to find out later that the bracken fern actually contains two poisons, one of which imitates the effects of radiation poisoning. And research has established that the high incidence of stomach cancer among the Japanese can probably be attributed to the popularity of bracken fern shoots in their diet. We steered well clear of the bracken.

What we found in abundance was sword fern. This would come in handy, we were told, if we wanted to weave a floor mat. Or line a pit oven. But that was not our mission.

The ostrich was obviously the fern of choice. The problem

was, as our guidebook pointed out, the ostrich fern is more likely to be found in the Interior of British Columbia. A quick check confirmed the obvious: we were a long way away from the Interior.

Our options were narrowing. We circled the sword fern warily, debating our chances. Nothing said *not* to eat it. It did bear a sort of distant-relation resemblance to the ostrich variety. And as long as we avoided the bracken, we decided, we'd probably be okay.

After twenty minutes, with two baskets full, we went our separate ways, promising to report back after an experimental tasting.

It took about an hour to peel half a dozen. They did not yield easily. They were very furry and I don't fancy a mouthful of anything with fur on it. I plunged them in boiling water, rinsed them, and set them on to boil a second time, then a third. I forget where I'd read to do that but it seemed a sensible precaution as I wanted to dilute the fuzz effect as thoroughly as possible.

My fiddleheads looked exactly as they should. Exactly, I was sure, as those set before the queen. I slathered them with butter and they looked even better. A dash of salt, a squirt of lemon—voilà! I dug in.

Steven Hawking talks about the trillionth trillionth of the trillionth particle of the split second in which the world was begat. I suspect I discovered a time frame many times more minuscule than that. The fiddleheads exploded from my mouth like something shot from a high-powered rifle, catapulted through the open door, across the deck and into the cedars beyond.

Bitter doesn't really capture the full impact of that first brutal contact. I remember fuzz. I remember something akin to what I suspect iodine might taste like. I remember my mouth closing in on itself, cheeks snapped together like pads of Velcro, then the dive for the water tap.

I bathed my mouth in a restorative gin and tonic and called my friend with an update.

Cleverly, she had waited until I had seen things through at this end.

"Good thinking," I said. "What are friends for, after all?"

I still harbour a hankering for fiddleheads. I still probe the papery nests of last year's fronds in search of the new shoots poking through. There is still a romance attached to it all that I can't quite shake. But I now gather my fiddleheads in a frozen block at the grocery store and leave the foraging to others.

Februarys are steeped in grey. My favourite walks have turned to mush, I've run out of ways to serve squash and even the dog sleeps in. But the day I pick my first nettle is the day I know that I'll make it through till the flowering currant blooms again and the hummingbirds return.

Stinging nettles are the first of nature's garden greens to challenge winter's chill. Plucky and exuberant and against all odds they emerge from the cold soil and grow like weeds. They've long been treated like weeds as well, which is really quite unfair because not only are they good food and good medicine, they are the source of all manner of amusing and quirky diversions for a dreary February day.

You must be alert when picking nettles. There's an old proverb that describes the recommended technique: *If you gently touch a nettle it will sting you for your pains; grasp it like a lad of mettle, and as soft as silk remains.*

I've seen the mettlesome nettler at work. He leaps in bare handed, seizes the plant's tender top in a firm grip and snaps it off, unscathed. I have tried this go-for-the-throat approach. It doesn't work. Hands on fire, you thrash about in search of dock leaves to rub on your seared flesh. (Mother Nature, ever thoughtful, keeps the antidote close by.)

Or you can fight fire with fire: they say that if you rub a nettle rash with nettle juice the prickly sting will disappear. Which, to my mind, is a bit like applying a branding iron to a burn. I don't endorse that theory either. I wear gloves.

The word *nettle,* by the way, comes from the Anglo-Saxon word for "needle," a reference to the hypodermic-like action of the millions of tiny hairs that cover the leaves and stem. Each hair harbours a compound containing acetylcholine, histamine and formic acid—the latter being the same stinging venom behind the painful bite of the red ant. The skin immediately erupts in itchy red weals that can last several days. I try to avoid this unpleasantness if at all possible, although, in the deep gloom of February, even weal-watching has a certain allure.

Yet I love nettles with a passion. I love gathering them. I love their high-test, earthy taste, which is sort of like chard, sort of like spinach—only more so. And I love the Zen of the whole nettle experience, from patch to pot.

I've always imagined that my particular little corner of heaven will feature an endless beach, sea-to-sky books and

24/7 pizza delivery. Then every year, as regular as rain, I remember what I've missed and revise that fantasy. Heaven is the sun on your back, a dog at your side and a nettle patch you can call your own.

My personal patch is in a ferny hollow, just beyond the holly bush where the sun sifts through the alders and the chick-adees hang out. We—my dog and I—go to the lake first so he can roll in the goose poop and check out the buffleheads courting by the shore. Then we head back to the alder grove.

The marvellous and, to me, miraculous thing about this prickly plant is that its arrival seems orchestrated to coincide with the time we need it most. Nettles are loaded with iron, the very thing our bodies crave in the doldrums of winter's last days. They also contain serotonin, which, according to Kevin Spelman, an Ayurvedic teacher and herbalist, proba-bly explains the sense of renewal and well-being we experi-ence when we treat ourselves to this natural pick-me-up. Nettles have been used to cure all manner of ills—asthma, fevers, arthritis, gout. It's been said that the Roman legions, on duty in England, relied on nettles to treat the aches and pains brought on by the damp and cold.

Other ancient rites associated with nettles might also be of some interest to those in search of diversion on a rainy day. What you do, according to Roman custom, is pick yourself a sturdy bunch of nettles, take off your clothes and proceed to beat yourself silly, concentrating as well as you can through the burning pain on any area of the body in need of the net-tles' energizing medicine—a rheumatic hand, a creaky joint, whatever. One of the Romans' favourite forms of flagella-tion was to deliver vigorous sharp, stinging blows to the sub-navel area in order to heighten sexual potency. It's worth a try I suppose. Nettles are readily available. You don't need a prescription. And the procedure, though unorthodox, is entirely legal.

Since a good nettle thrashing isn't everybody's cup of tea, I suggest a more user-friendly stimulant: nettle soup. According to folklore, a Tibetan saint and poet named Milaraspa lived on the stuff for years. But then he didn't have a lot of choice. He lived in a cave. He meditated. He had loftier matters on his mind than what to cook for dinner. In the end, Milaraspa turned green and died. We're not told how long he lived or how he died but the fact that he died dyed is easily explained: chlorophyll. Nettles are loaded with it. I steamed a batch recently and set it to drain in a colander lined with paper towels. Within hours the paper had turned an intense, neon-bright green. Milaraspa green. A shade rather better suited to plants than people.

I quite fancy the idea of a mood-altering substance that is free for the picking and good for you too. And it delights me to think that, even though the saintly Milaraspa went to his death in a colour unbecoming, he went peacefully, in his nettle patch, blissed out on Nature's own Prozac.

Here are two of my favourite things to do with nettles: soup and "nesto"—the nettle lover's version of pesto. Note: These recipes contain serotonin which has been known to trigger feelings of intense euphoria in some people. So dig in. And be glad!

Nesto

I love this primitive pesto. It's pungent and earthy and the deepest, wildest green imaginable. It's marvellous on spaghetti, linguine or any ribbon pasta. You can skim it on thin rounds of oil-smeared toast. It's good with goat cheese in an omelet. Or in a quiche with roasted peppers and shallots. If nettles don't grow where you live I offer my condolences.

4 cups firmly packed fresh young nettle leaves
2 cloves garlic, chopped
3 tablespoons pine nuts (or chopped walnuts)
½ teaspoon salt
½ cup extra-virgin olive oil
½ cup freshly grated Parmesan cheese
3 tablespoons softened butter

Using kitchen tongs, or with gloved hands, place the nettles in a steamer basket set over boiling water. Steam for 3 to 4 minutes, until well wilted, then put them in a colander to drain. Chop roughly and put them in the bowl of your food processor.

Add the garlic, nuts, salt and oil and whiz it all up until it's smooth. Add the cheese and butter and process again, briefly, until everything is well incorporated. If you think the sauce is too thick at this stage you can add a couple of tablespoons of boiling water and give it one more whirl. Makes enough for four big appetites, or 1 pound of pasta.

The Soup of Saints

This is essentially spinach soup with attitude. In fact, you can substitute spinach for the nettles if you must. Just bear in mind that you'll forfeit your saintly aura if you do.

8 cups firmly packed fresh young nettle leaves

2 tablespoons butter, plus an additional nub to stir in
  before serving (optional)

2 tablespoons extra-virgin olive oil

¾ cup each chopped celery, leeks and onions

6 cups good chicken stock (preferably homemade)

4 medium boiling potatoes, peeled and diced

¾ cup table cream

Salt and pepper

Using kitchen tongs, or with gloved hands, place the nettles in a steamer basket set over boiling water. Steam for 3 to 4 minutes, until well wilted, then put them in a colander to drain.

Melt the butter with the oil in a heavy saucepan over medium heat and gently cook the leeks, onions and celery until they are soft but not browned (about fifteen minutes). Add the nettles, stir to combine well, then add the stock. Bring the mixture to a boil and add the potatoes. Reduce heat and simmer gently until the potatoes are tender (about 45 minutes).

Purée in small batches in your food processor or using an immersion blender. Return the soup to the pan and add the cream along with salt and pepper to taste. Reheat the soup gently and whisk in a nugget of butter—a welcome bit of decadence—before serving.

Serves 6.

Good Things from the Valley

I'm in four-wheel drive. At summer's end the road, deep in dust and topsy-turvy at the best of times, is like some derelict roller coaster. Passing this way one day last spring, I'd stopped to let a mother goose and her seven wispy-feathered goslings cross, heading for a dip in the beaver pond. Today it's a blue heron who commandeers the right of way. I stop this time too and watch until it alights on a snag in the pond's centre. Beside me Dexter the dog huffs impatiently, and I move on.

We're not foraging today. We're going grocery shopping. This time, though, I'm not heading for the pretty little local stores where all roads on the Island—the paved ones, at any rate—lead. Today is an off-road shopping experience, my weekly trip to a five-acre market garden, a valley of living green, sunlight and birdsong. Dexter sits at attention, alert to every lurch and pothole. He loves a shopping trip, this one especially. Here, there's a pond smack in the middle of the apple display. And a dog named Lucy to go swimming with.

Lucy, in her capacity as official greeter, announces our

arrival. My friend the gardener and personal produce consultant meets us by the arbour where the kiwis grow. We make our way past peppers and basil to the blackberry aisle. It's steep, a tunnel of bramble, which we navigate by way of wooden steps and a shaded hairpin path that takes us to the valley. The berries are pretty much finished now but a few weeks ago you could have filled a bucket here without ever moving from the third step.

At the end of the path we're under the apple trees—Gravensteins, Galas, Mutsus, Russets, Kings. There are pear trees too, and plums. So much fruit I think the trees must surely double over with the weight. I decide on Gravensteins and—from the plum department—Bradshaw, Burbank, Victoria and a Japanese variety that sit in my hand like small dark jewels.

From somewhere on the wooded hill comes the shy *tsk-tsk* of a chickadee. And as we pause to listen, squinting into the sun, a passing raven calls to us and we hear the soft quick breath-sounds of his wings. No Muzak here.

The dogs career past us through a corridor of bulrushes and into the pond. They paddle in circles, through duckweed and around water lilies, and when they scramble up the bank to shake their coats they fling rainbows into the air. We stop to inspect the lettuce. I want two and I ponder, briefly, the colour scheme. Burgundy, I think. That one—the wine-red oakleaf. And something in green, a baby Bibb perhaps, to set it off. There. I've composed, on the spot, an impeccably accessorized salad.

Beyond the salad bar are chard, cauliflower and broccoli. My friend pulls aside a massive fan of leaves to reveal a cauliflower as big as a basketball, snow white and perfect in its snug green shawl. This is too much cauliflower for me. I opt for the chard.

She points to the quinoa, red hoops of it, ready for harvest. Bees thrum amongst the mint that grows, fragrant and waist high, all around us. And there's more mint over there, beyond the potato patch and the soldierly rows of corn. She stoops to pull carrots.

Another aisle, this time nature's pharmacy: echinacea, with its pink tailored petals and huge thistle-like seed pods. Then, our footsteps whispering in the dry grass, we stroll past the sold-out raspberry canes to the path through the cedars that takes us back up the hill.

A few impulse purchases are made, as always, at the place on the porch where money changes hands—a jar of crabapple jelly this time, and cherry tomatoes, chubby and sweet, which I select by the handful, like candy. As I leave I pause in the shade of the fig tree and dig deep into my bag for a Gravenstein to eat on the way home.

I can't buy a butterflied pork chop in my shop in the valley. I can't use a debit card. Or get my bacon sliced just so. I have to settle for a leisurely stroll, with romping dogs, through avenues of fruit trees and aisles of plenty while my next meal is pulled from the ground. People (not-from-here people, that is) wonder how I manage without a bank, paved parking lots, a mall. How in the world I possibly get by without access to a hangar full of food stacked in crates to the ceiling. Where wieners can be had in 20-pound case loads and the coleslaw comes pre-cut in neat plastic bags.

Oh well, I say, I manage. Somehow. And after all, a city,

should I need one, is just a ferry ride away. But the truth is, if they could shop where I shop, even once, they wouldn't have to ask.

Just down the road from my grocer-in-the-valley live the chickens who deliver the eggs I love to eat. One morning a few years ago when I had dropped by to pick up my weekly dozen I asked Nancy, their adopted mom and manager, if I could meet them.

These "girls," which is how Nancy refers to them, are drop-dead gorgeous. A cross of Rhode Island Red and Barred Plymouth Rock, they're sleek and plump and impeccably groomed, like matrons decked out for a tea party. Some were hard at work when I got there, hunkered dreamily in private places doing what a girl's got to do. I blew them a kiss and turned my attention to the dozen or so who were bustling fretfully about inspecting my yellow rubber boots.

I complimented them on their exquisite get-ups. Feathers the colour of . . . what? Black, at first glance, then registering a burnished bronze, a green highlight here and there as the sun licked their backs. They seemed unaware of their beauty. They just burbled and babbled, sharing the news— *We have a visitor!* They seemed somewhat skeptical about the yellow footgear, poking critically, cocking their heads as if sizing up this audacious fashion statement.

What did they eat? I asked, for surely here was the secret. Melon rinds. Fruit of all kinds. Greens, pasta, raisins, cracked corn, whole wheat, sunflower seeds and porridge—

they love porridge. If chickens could burp appreciative burps these chickens surely would.

Their back door opens into the forest, discreetly fenced, with lots of room to waddle and poke. Here they find insects, juicy little bugs and other crawly things—Nature's own al fresco buffet. When I went out they followed, anxious not to miss a thing, strutting about like grande dames through a stately home as if to say, *And here, on your left, under the cedar is where we hang out when it rains. And on your right, the mossy mat that catches the sun at noon.*

"Lovely," I said, "a beautiful place you've got here."

This is chicken heaven. A far cry from the assembly-line life of your average chicken, stuffed into tiny cages where their sole job is to eat and lay. Their days and seasons are cleverly manipulated to achieve the optimum monotony necessary for efficient production. They are given names like Leghorn No. 2988. No Ann or Zena like the girls I met on that autumn morning. And, in the bleak world of the anonymous chicken, whoever you are, you're never good enough. Breeders are continually messing about to find an even better chicken to take your place—one that matures faster, eats less, lays more eggs and delivers a fatter profit. The hen is an egg machine and, for the most part, is treated with the diligence due any useful machine: just keep it running. Niceties are wasted on machines. As Samuel Butler said, "A hen is only an egg's way of making another egg."

In the high-density, high-performance world of competitive chickenhood, all the nurturing duties—feeding, watering, egg gathering and cleaning—are performed by machines. None of this mawkish bonding with your human caretakers. No gentle fingers combing through sleek feathers here. No cheery "Good morning, girls" as the henhouse door swings open on another day. I know that a hen's brain is approximately the size of a pea and that their needs seem to us to be simple in the extreme. Yet what living thing does not respond to kindness and a loving touch?

These particular chickens obviously do. These are enormously happy. You can see it in their strut. Hear it in their warble and cluck. They like the life they lead and the job they've been given to do. The proof is in the egg.

It is brown, heavy in the hand. Broken into a buttered frying pan, the bright yolk stands high, its white skirt gathered tidily around it. Poached, they emerge from their hot-water bath tucked into neat bundles that sit like two tiny, perfect pillows on a slice of toast.

I traded my empty egg carton for a full one, thanked Nancy and the girls for welcoming me into their midst, and noticed as I headed home that several of the eggs I'd eat when I got there were still warm.

The Rainforest Tea Ceremony

I count my blessings. I have, I figure, more than my fair share. High on the list is my time with me and a good cup of tea. It was the nineteenth-century gastronome Anthelme Brillat-Savarin who said: "Tell me what you eat and I will tell you what you are." Would he agree, I wonder, that equally revealing is how one takes tea? I'd like to think so.

Polished silver, china cups, and the flocking together of women in fancy hats were all part of the civilized tea ritual in my mother's day. As a young lady-child I was expected to wear special clothes and work the room with trays of pin-wheel sandwiches, a duty I assumed with suspect good grace as I got to eat all the olives I could snitch.

These days, for tea-with-me, dress is casual, shoes are optional and, despite Samuel Johnson's claim that "tea time is any time that tea is served," my countdown starts at four. Water boils on the stove. My teapot, an elegantly proportioned thing of beauty fashioned by a local potter, stands by waiting to be warmed. I reach not for the fine china—there is none—but for my favourite mug. It is squat and heavy and fits my encircling hands as no delicate Balique cup ever could or ever was intended to. Two spoonfuls into the tea ball: I like a robust brew. And when it has steeped (three minutes, no more, no less) I move to the saggy old chair by the window, dislodge the cats and settle in. If it's teatime with cookies (McVitie's gingersnaps are good) the dog joins me. He too likes them dunked. That's it: just my dog and me and a nice cup of tea.

I've tried other variations on the teatime theme. I've been treated, as noted, to the scones and jam and clotted-cream experience, which I'll happily revisit next time I pass through Devon. I've done tea-and-Styrofoam courtesy of food-court vendors. I've even had tea at the Empress Hotel in Victoria, which was a grand, if pricey, affair. But there is one tea moment that can happen only when there's love in the air and the planets are aligned just so. It's called The Birders' Rainforest Tea Ceremony. It is my favourite by far—less ceremony, really, than serendipitous interlude.

A company of eight, we'd gathered at a forest rendezvous to drink in the morning and spy on the birds. We stood transfixed at the sound of a Swainson's thrush. We heard song sparrows, towhees, orange-crowned warblers, winter wrens and nuthatches. We watched as a crossbill bathed in a pond, then preened fussily on the bough of an alder. We saw an olive-sided flycatcher nab its prey against the hot blue backscape of the sky. Then somebody mentioned tea.

Tea? Why not? There it was, right at our feet, by the gravelly path where we stood: a herb of the mint family called yerba buena. When you crush its leaves between your fingers you breathe in the promise of what's to come—pungent, like mint, with hints of smoke and spice. The Saanich and the Halq'emeylem peoples used it for tea. They'd crush it too and rub it on their skin to disguise their human scent when hunting deer. San Francisco was once called Yerba Buena. It means, aptly enough, "good plant," and that good plant was soon steeping in a fat brown teapot—lidless—at my elbow.

We had left the bluffs we'd explored that morning and followed a fellow birder to his cabin in the valley below. It was a Hobbit-like structure with a mossy roof and walls swaddled in ivy and periwinkle. A rudimentary sundial etched into the cedar siding told us the time: a shadow-slice past noon.

We sat outside on wooden benches, our tea room a green-draped grove where butterflies danced. The resident cat lolled in a patch of sun by a cedar stump. Beyond the tea-grove the grass grew waist high. And the birds sang.

Kip-kip-kip . . . eight pairs of ears prick to attention at the sound. Siskins? Crossbills? The consensus is crossbills. We nod sagely and go back to our tea.

And that . . . ?

Zee-zee-zeetsi-dee-diddle-iddle-dee! The white-crowned sparrow. Of course.

And that? A junco? No, no—an orange-crowned warbler, surely. The cat rolls over and blinks at the sky. Small talk is not required when birders share a cuppa in the woods. But, as with any civilized gathering, even here in our rainforest tea room, certain rules apply.

Rule No. 1 among birders at tea is never to say of a robin "It's just a robin." "Just a" *anything* is bad form, for that matter. Birder etiquette demands equal reverence for all. Seagulls included. Rule No. 2: no blurting. A thin *peep-peep* from the forest canopy should be assessed with caution, a guarded "Hmm," no more—unless you're very sure. Ill-considered guesswork like "Turkey vulture," say, or "Sharp-shinned hawk" could have awkward repercussions: silence, foot shuffles, noncommittal squints into the middle distance and—I've seen this happen—great spluttering and spewing out of hot tea signalling a birder gaffe beyond forgiving. Best to let someone else take the lead here while you test the wind and fall in agreeably where appropriate.

Otherwise, you can kick back, relax and let nature take its course. Which it will, without fail, when you're in the company of people who've discovered, like you, the magic of wild tea and birdsong under the cedars.

Some People

My enchantment with the peculiar charms of Island life was not, I discovered to my amazement, shared by everyone who came our way. Yerba buena is not everybody's cup of tea. Wild mushrooms can be, let's face it, too scary for words. Dried sea lettuce and homemade blackberry wine get mixed reviews.

We'd become accustomed, over the years, to visits by comparative strangers: friends of friends, Uncle Arnie's nephew by marriage, a former neighbour's daughter's boyfriend. They came our way because they were curious. What *was* this place? And why in the world would anyone choose to live here? *Besides,* they'd say, *we just happened to be in the neighbourhood*—which, I should point out, is a bit like just happening upon Joe Batt's Arm, Newfoundland, which is not exactly on the way to anywhere either.

We welcomed them all. Even the Grimlys, whom we'd known only slightly from long-ago summers in Ontario cottage country. They arrived for lunch, a party of four: Mama Grimly, Papa Grimly and two pale, twenty-something junior Grimlys. It was a soft summer day, that idyllic time of year when the garden's bounty was ripe for the picking, and I entered into an orgy of hospitality that would have brought Martha Stewart to her knees.

I'd been dabbling in the precarious art of bagel making that summer, a rather messy business until you get the hang of things, which I hadn't quite. Nevertheless, I'd made some that morning. They were oddly shaped, only vaguely bagel-ish, but they were fragrant and chewy and I served them anyway. We had cheese—Asiago, Gorgonzola and a creamy chèvre from the Okanagan Valley. There were homemade dills and pickled beets. Tomatoes too, still warm from the sun, which I'd sliced and layered in a bath of olive oil and fresh basil. There was a bowl of mixed greens—red-leaf lettuce, arugula, radicchio—and a garlicky vinaigrette. We had fresh-pressed apple juice and a smorgasbord of beers. A peach pie waited in the wings.

I have an elegant coffee-table book called *Monet's Table*. It is filled with dreamy sun-shot images of Monet's home in Giverny, of linen-draped tables laden with fresh figs and wheels of Brie and Veuve Clicquot champagne set to cool in oak buckets. My table wasn't a patch on Monet's. But it was inviting nevertheless. I waved everyone to their seats, noting a certain reluctance on the part of the Grimly contingent as they shuffled to their places. I put it down to shyness and urged them to dig in.

"Drinks? Beer? Apple juice?" I clucked about, exuding cheer.

"No, nothing thanks," chorused the Grimlys, glumly.

I snapped open a beer for myself and reached for a bagel. It was good. As were the dill pickles, which exploded with such a commotion between my ears that, for several minutes, I failed to notice the silence that had settled around the table. No one was eating but me. Oh, Chris was of course. He's always an enthusiastic tablemate, but our guests were sitting over nearly empty plates.

Mr. Grimly was picking the poppy seeds off a bagel. His

wife was fishing through the salad bowl like someone rooting for scraps worth salvaging from a bin at a rummage sale. And the more emaciated of the young Grimly duo asked if I had any margarine.

"Sorry," I said. "Just butter."

She murmured something about low-density lipids and jammed arteries and pondered her naked bagel. I had by this time ploughed through a plateful of just about everything on offer. But otherwise little had been touched.

"You're not hungry," I noted.

"Oh it's not that," said Mrs. Grimly. "It's just that, well . . . we're not partial to vegetables."

"I don't mind broccoli," ventured Mr. Grimly helpfully.

"And cheese is so bad for you," added the missus.

"It gives me gas," said he.

"So. What *do* you eat?" I asked.

"Cheerios," said the junior member with the butter phobia.

"Ice cream," said Mr. Grimly.

"Well then," I said. "Ice cream it is."

I bundled the lot of them into the car and we went to the neighbourhood ice-cream parlour for double cones all round. I graciously let them pay. And I discreetly avoided pointing out the obvious corollary between two scoops of butterscotch swirl and instant cholesterol meltdown.

Afterwards, I suggested a beach walk. They looked dubious as I went into my chirpy tour-guide mode with promises of eagle sightings and frolicking seals and plenty of rest stops along the way. The Grimlys demurred. They weren't really walkers *per se,* they announced. They'd worn the wrong shoes, you see. The sun was too bright. The rocks too slippery. And the missus had an ice-cream headache. So we sat, six bumps on a sun-bleached log, while I dreamed sweet dreams of the unbroached peach pie waiting for me at home.

3

Who's That Klutz in My Kitchen?

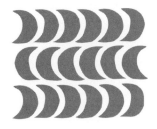

*There's nothing more dispiriting
than an orderly kitchen.*

LANDON SHAMBLES

The Accidental Cook

Julia Child and I have a lot in common. As Craig Claiborne put it, Julia was not born "with a wooden spoon in her mouth." Nor was I. She learned how to cook because she fell in love with a man who loved good food. Me too. She was also accident prone, another endearing quality we share.

For years pancakes stumped her because she had trouble cooking with eggs. She forgot to prick a duck's skin before cooking and the thing exploded in the oven. She dropped stuff—foodstuff—on the floor in front of a nationwide television audience. She didn't miss a beat. She promptly scooped it up (*They'll never notice*) and carried on. Once, when she ran out of butter while making a béarnaise sauce, she blithely substituted lard and was dumbfounded when the "sauce" morphed into a brick at the table. And when asked for her favourite comfort food she didn't hesitate: "Red meat and gin."

You see? She's just like me. Except, of course, that Julia pulled herself together. I didn't. She became an accomplished chef, beloved by millions. I'm still working on lump-free gravy.

But it was the Windex-enhanced-Italian-bread incident that inspired me to undertake the study I did. I was curious to know whether random acts of spectacular stupidity were a purely local phenomenon, or whether they occur with comparable frequency in kitchens other than mine. The Windex incident, by the way, is easily explained. I was baking bread—big fat rounds of peasant-style Italian bread—and because I like a strong crust, when the loaves go in the oven I mist them with water. The thing is, my bread-misting spray bottle is kept conveniently at hand along with a collection of cleaning materials—Comet, Goo-Gone, Mr. Clean and such like. The Windex spritzer looks very much like the bread-misting spritzer. I picked the wrong one, okay? Accidents happen.

But did they happen to everybody? Was I the only klutz on the loose out there?

I needn't have worried. I discovered, to my great delight, a vast secret society of culinary misfits, each with a story to tell. Some of the perpetrators are personal friends, so names have been withheld to protect them from their families. And be warned: some of their stories will make your teeth itch. Here are the highlights.

First up, a tale very similar to my Windex adventure: a woman is preparing Swiss steak. She reaches for the cooking oil, and as the beef sizzles in the pan she detects an unexpected but oddly familiar smell. She ignores it. The Swiss steak is brought to the table. Her husband eats. Then, suddenly and with a strangulated cry, he spits. That he did so was a very good thing. The beef had been sizzled in Pine-Sol.

Another among the nameless and accident prone fed her guests dumplings studded with dead bugs. An honest mistake, really. How could she possibly have known that those tiny corpses were interred in the jar that contained the dill that went into the dumplings that everyone gobbled up so appreciatively? Heavens. It could happen to anyone.

Then there are the various found objects excavated from the cavities of countless Christmas turkeys. It's an impressive list: bags of giblets, wine corks, earrings, cooking instructions, elastic bands and, in one memorable instance, a few yards of rather greasy, but done-to-a-turn, paper towel.

Someone even confessed to boiling up a length of dressmaker's tape with the spinach.

One friend created a novel dish for company that she later dubbed Crest Chicken. She sensed something was amiss almost immediately. Her guests had fallen silent. Knives and forks were being routed, with painstaking precision, around the elegantly stuffed chicken breasts in a game attempt to salvage a meal of glazed carrots and rice. Why? The chicken tasted like toothpaste. Mint-flavoured Crest toothpaste. The same mouthwash mintiness as the mint-flavoured toothpicks she'd used to skewer the chicken breasts as they cooked.

Then there's me. My personal repertoire of culinary embarrassments spans several decades. However, it is usually on the occasion of the Dinner Party that my skills regress to most spectacular effect. There was the time I set fire to an elaborate centrepiece of dried flowers at a dinner for twelve. I had already burned the roast and was lighting the candles when flame met petrified lily. Fortunately our guests had the presence of mind to fling glasses of wine into the inferno, and we soldiered on without further incident.

On another occasion, on a curry kick this time, Chris and I created an entire meal from a cookbook we'd not used before. We knew better. The main course was murgh makkhani, a lightly spiced chicken dish that, in Indian restaurants, comes in an exotic glow-in-the-dark pink. We try to avoid pink food as a rule, so when this recipe delivered chunks of sickly white chicken in what looked very much like wallpaper paste, I took it in stride. Unfortunately, the rice was white as well. As was the potato-cauliflower combo, aloo gobi. The plates on which I heaped this white-on-white collaboration were, as luck would have it, an even whiter shade of white. We introduced this monochromatic ensemble as a theme meal, passed the wine (white) and announced that if anyone would like to order pizza we would be more than amenable. Nobody did. They stared in fascination at the pale offering set before them and did what any well-mannered guest's got to do: they ate without complaint and left soon afterwards.

Then there were the houseguests whose visit coincided with an occasion of particular import for me: the harvesting of my garlic. I love garlic. When garlic beckons, garlic rules our days.

At lunch I set out tzatziki (a garlicky yogurt and cucumber dip) and ate most of it myself. Our guests opted for stark naked pita bread, which struck me as odd, but they enjoyed several helpings of avgolemono (a lemony Greek soup), which, through a dreadful oversight on my part, happened to be 100 percent garlic free. At dinner the lamb, bristling with garlic, was greeted with muted praise. It wasn't until Day Three that the penny dropped.

I'd made a potato salad. With garlic. Whole cloves of garlic, a dozen or more, had been slow-simmered with tiny new potatoes, bathed in olive oil and balsamic vinegar and tossed with handfuls of fresh basil. But by this time my passion was meeting with organized and visible resistance. Telltale heaps of untouched garlic were being steadily stockpiled on each guest's plate. Wisely, I said nothing. Wisely, nor did they.

They've not been back, not in garlic season anyway. Too bad. I think they would have enjoyed, perhaps even applauded, the story of the one that got away . . .

I was on the back porch, in the high heat of July, with a scattering of garlic at my feet. This is garlic I grew myself, another mini-milestone in my late-blooming career as a gardener. The heads, fifteen of them, are the size of cherry tomatoes. The idea is this: I will rescue my puny harvest by turning it into a home-fashion statement. I am going to make a braid.

I've chosen a shady spot for this project, a catch-all corner housing a jumble of umbrellas, rubber boots and running shoes. In a clearing amidst this clutter sits my garlic. My how-to guide sits at my feet, open to the page entitled "Braiding Garlic Made Easy." However, since I'm a tad shortsighted, the all-important instructions sit at the fuzzy periphery of my range of vision.

On the wall in front of me is a hook from which I've suspended, as per the instructions, a loop of strong twine. So far so good. Next:

"Select a garlic bulb and tie the stem securely to the end of the loop of twine."

I should point out that I'm not particularly good at this sort of thing. Positioning Tab A into Slot B to construct a Batmobile from the back of a cereal box would present an insurmountable challenge. But I've braided hair so I can surely braid garlic. Besides, having steered the project to this stage since planting time last October, I am determined to see it through. I squint down at the instructions: there's a diagram to illustrate the process.

The bottom of the loop is raised to form two auxiliary loops, creating three possible paths for the garlic stalk to negotiate. I weave the stem past string A, through the loop, around string B and pull. The garlic slips its noose and falls to my feet. I begin again. Into the loop, around the string, out of the loop and back again. I tug. Garlic No. 1 is now in position. I bend to read the instructions for the next step.

"Select a second garlic bulb and weave the stem first over the right string, then over the left string. Next, weave the stem back over the right string, pull tight, and when it's secure move it into position by bulb No. 1."

The diagram that accompanies this gibberish looks like an illustration of the lower intestine that you find in medical textbooks. But never mind. This proves to be a fleeting problem because, as my powers of recall are in the same advanced state of decline as my eyesight, by the time I resume my stance at the weaving string I've forgotten it all anyway.

I abandon my how-to guide. I can't read and braid at the same time so I'm going to have to rely on my wits and improvise. This is precarious territory. I've now got two lengths of string, a loop and two stalks of garlic to manipulate, and no obvious strategy is presenting itself. I plunge in anyway, and after much bobbing and weaving end up in an untidy arrangement of limbs, twine, thumbs and garlic stalks. At this point garlic No. 2 slithers out of bounds and ends up in a yellow gumboot. The mercury is at 28° Celsius and climbing.

I have a friend who grows garlic the size of baseballs and weaves them into magnificent braids in three minutes flat. I call her and order one. Extra large. Price no object. Then I fish my crop out of the boot pile, tie it up with the string and hang it at a jaunty angle from the pot rack in the kitchen.

I'm philosophical. This was obviously a particularly balky, braid-averse strain of garlic that was never intended to be a home-fashion accessory in the first place. This garlic was destined for a 350°F oven, to be baked whole and smeared liberally over thick slices of chewy Italian bread. And I, with my severely challenged hand-eye capabilities, was meant to eat and enjoy.

Avgolemono Soup

Avgolemono, translated from the Greek, means "egg-lemon," and when it comes to soup nothing could be simpler. It's lovely hot but I much prefer it cold, served in chilled bowls on a steamy summer day: an elegant soup in the best of taste—despite the regrettable absence of garlic.

6 cups chicken stock (preferably homemade but a commercial broth works fine too)

½ cup long-grain (basmati) white rice

3 egg yolks

4 tablespoons fresh-squeezed lemon juice

Salt and pepper

Thinly sliced lemon for garnish

Heat the stock to boiling and add the rice. Simmer, covered, for 20 minutes or until the rice is just tender. While the rice cooks, whisk together the egg yolks and lemon juice in a small bowl.

When the rice is ready, remove the pot from the heat and slowly whisk a cup of the hot broth into the egg mixture. Whisk the contents of the bowl back into the soup, increase the heat to medium and stir constantly until the soup is hot. Don't let it boil. Remove from the heat, add salt and pepper to taste and serve garnished with a lemon slice.

If you plan to serve it cold, let the soup come to room temperature, cover and refrigerate.

Serves 6.

Why Dumb Things Happen to Smart People

Part of my problem, and I admit to this belatedly, is sheer perversity: an insistence, against all logic, on a course of action that's doomed to failure. I think of Julia and her lard-laced béarnaise. That little voice—I'm sure she heard it—that whispered *No, Julia, no! Not the lard!* goes unheeded. If lard's what you've got then lard's what you use. You thumb your nose at reason and keep your fingers crossed.

Perversity is what led to my sticky standoff with James Beard and the mess with florentines.

There are two kinds of florentines. There's James's version—a rich, chewy, candy-like cookie with a coating of chocolate on one side. And there's mine—a rock-hard cookie lookalike that, when baked, adheres with the tenacity of Krazy Glue to all cookware surfaces. These are typically served up (a) in shards pried loose with sharp blows of a kitchen cleaver or (b) as florentine dust—the residue remaining after the cleaver attack.

My travails in florentine territory began several years ago. The fact that things went horribly wrong is attested to by an anguished scrawl (*Aaaaarrrgh!!*) in red ink—or blood?—in the margin of my recipe book *The New James Beard*.

Nevertheless, I came to the task the second time around brimming with confidence. I knew precisely where I'd gone wrong before and I was hardly likely to make the same mistake twice. Nor did I. I found a whole new way to do it wrong.

James's recipe involves a heart-stopping combination of cream, sugar, butter, corn syrup, nuts, candied peel—every single item on the list of X-rated foods identified by your doctor at your last cholesterol checkup. All of this is now boiled up till it reaches the soft-ball stage, whereupon we are instructed to deposit it, by sticky spoon-loads, onto a baking sheet. A baking sheet lined with parchment paper.

I don't have parchment paper. What I have is waxed

paper, which is what I used before and which is why my florentines sported shiny, permanently affixed, inedible waxed paper bottoms.

So, older now and wiser by far from that experience, I sidled up to James with an alternative proposal. How about, in the absence of parchment, I just slather the pans—Teflon coated—with lots and lots of vegetable oil? That should work. Right? Of course it should, said I, thinking, "He's the chef—why didn't he think of this?"

I boiled up the lethal ingredients. I spooned them out on grease-slicked Teflon. They baked for the requisite ten minutes and sat to cool.

My first attempt to coax a cookie from its miracle no-stick perch was met with steely resistance. I reversed the spatula for greater leverage and went into excavation mode. Nothing budged. They were glued there. I went at them with the cleaver (recently sharpened) and was still stymied. I took the pan outside, snuck up on it from the rear and laid into it with my steel-toed hiking boots. *Biff. Thwack. Bam.* This got me nowhere. I had discovered an adhesive that could make me millions. But there was no way I was going to extricate even one florentine.

I filled a laundry tub and immersed the entire mess in hot soapy water. The next day I retrieved the pan, re-engaged the spatula and washed eighteen soggy florentines down the drain.

I have jotted down some advice to myself in the margins of my James Beard cookbook. *Warning! Leave this area immediately. Go directly to Chinese Chews—page 486.*

Another option—a novel idea—is to follow the instructions.

Cooking by the Book

I have at least eighty-five cookbooks. I don't need eighty-five cookbooks, of course. No one *needs* eighty-five of anything. I collect them because I find it impossible not to.

My cookbooks fall into five categories.

There's the Not on a Bet section, a testament to the lure of remainder tables and yard sales visited over the years. If I paid a dollar for any one of them I paid too much. The most spectacular example of pennies misspent would have to be *Benedicamus Domino,* compiled by the good ladies of St. Margaret's Church, King's Lynn, Norfolk. This is an astonishing collection of curiosities, none of them edible to my way of thinking, the bulk of which are puddings: pages and pages of suggestions on how to combine flour, candied peel and currants with generous lashings of lard. And then there's faggots—little balls of ground-up pig's liver, suet and breadcrumbs, which may or may not be absolutely delicious. I'll never know. And Norfolk rusks. You remember rusks: we used to insert them into the mouths of teething babies to dam up the drool.

Then there's my Library of Noble Intentions. Here are titles like *Quick and Easy Recipes to Lower your Cholesterol,* wherein are featured such delicacies as oat groats with carrot and parsley, and wheat germ prune muffins. *Modern Vegetarian Cookery* (circa 1967) offers up the likes of mashed-turnip-and-semolina gnocchi. And there's *The Gourmet Gazelle,* which, I must confess, got quickly buried under *Truffles and*

Other Treats so I never did discover the gazelle I might have been.

Here too sits Julia Child, a regal presence indeed, and my most noble of noble intentions. I stand in awe of Julia. She dedicated years to translating the finer points of French cookery for a Betty Crocker-besotted American public. She brought the likes of blanquette de veau and Charlotte aux pommes into our kitchens and made them feel right at home. But Julia was a grande dame with a more leisurely schedule than mine: her onion soup—rich, delicious, authentic through and through—is a three-hour commitment. A luxury I aspire to but that real life does not permit.

The bulk of shelf space is taken up by my Ethnic Explorer series—Mexican, Moroccan, Vietnamese, Thai, Greek, Italian, Caribbean, Brazilian, Indian. These are culinary travelogues that afford me hours of reading pleasure and little else. How often have I found myself thwarted for want of mung bean threads or tree ears or coconut sugar!

Amongst my Ethnic Explorer collection, in a corner reserved for repeat offenders, sits the most infuriating cookbook ever unleashed upon an impressionable public: *China Moon* by Barbara Tropp. Oh, the cover is irresistible, a triumph of hip graphics and sassy copy: Stir Fry Dancing Crab, Cosmic Chaos Soup, Yin Yang Tart. So clever! Who could resist?

But be warned! Ms. Tropp is a shameless tease. There is precious little in this ill-conceived repertoire that you can assemble without at least three months' lead time. Unless of course you happen to have a stock of infused oils and vinegars and all manner of eccentrically combined spices at hand at all times. It's a cunning strategy.

You see, Ms. Tropp owns the China Moon restaurant in San Francisco. So if you can't make it yourself, which is pretty much a foregone conclusion, you'll have to pay this wily marketeer to cook it for you.

Then there's the Archives, permanent home to our resident community of paper-eating silverfish. These are books that date back to my young-mom-at-home days, when helpmates like Peg Bracken's *I Hate to Cook Book* stood by with countless easy and affordable ways to combine hamburger or tuna fish with a can of soup and crushed potato chips. Peg Bracken hangs in there still, albeit in bits and pieces, but she's no longer relevant, as I now love to cook.

It's very easy to spot a good cookbook. Its years of loyal service are imprinted on every page. And when you cradle it in your hand it opens of its own accord to the juiciest bits inside.

I have an armload of favourites, books I love like family and couldn't live without. They are my Old Standbys. Closest to my heart are the books of M. F. K. Fisher. And although she shares a modest collection of recipes with us— *Addie's Quick Bucket Bread, Aunt Gwen's Fried Egg Sandwiches, cauliflower and cheese*—these are not cookbooks, they're food books. M. F. K. Fisher is the most writerly of food writers. Her words fairly shimmer, and her love for her subject suffuses every page. She writes about oysters, family dinners, how to boil rice and make a nice potato soup. She's wise and warm and, as James Beard once said, she "has the effect of sending the reader away with a desire to love better and live more fully." And that, say I, is exactly what a friend-in-the-kitchen is for.

My Old Standbys include a star-studded delegation from Italy: amongst them are Giuliano Bugialli (*The Fine Art of Italian Cooking*) and Marcella Hazan (*Essentials of Classic Italian Cooking*). I'm not sure how these two feel about being snugged up shoulder to shoulder on my kitchen shelf, but I'm extremely happy with the arrangement. It was to Giuliano I turned for my initiation into the opulent world of risottos. For my first osso buco I again took guidance from Giuliano. Marcella's instructions were daunting in the extreme: I'd have had to badger some butcher into swearing, on oath, that those veal shanks were indeed the *hind* shanks and nothing *but* the hind shanks so help me, God. I'd have had to hector him into cutting them just so (1½ inches thick, no more, no less). And he was not, upon pain of death, to remove the enveloping skin. I'm sure Marcella would have treated me to a fine osso buco. If I had had the chutzpah to see it through.

On the other hand, when I crave gnocchi it's Marcella's feather-light spinach and ricotta combo that seduces me every time. It was Marcella who inveigled me, against my better judgment, to concoct a pasta sauce with canned tuna and tomatoes—insisting, of course, on only the very best canned tuna (packed in oil and imported from Italy). That's when I knew we'd get along: I have been railing for years against the Miss Mew–style tuna fluff, packed in water, that masquerades as people food in our supermarkets. If you can find *good* canned tuna, firm fleshed and delectably oily, you too can be a Marcella convert.

Franco Galli and his *Il Fornaio Baking Book* rounds out my Italian contingent. We're pretty much inseparable, Franco and I, and have been for years. He took me under his wing and taught me how to make bread, real bread—big, fat, rough-hewn loaves with a crackling crust and dense, chewy crumb. Life without Galli is life without *pagnotta*, hardly worth the bother.

When I'm having an all-vegetable kind of day I turn, for inspiration and cheerful company, to *Sundays at Moosewood Restaurant*. My favourite soups, robust and inventively spiced, are Moosewood soups: Mariner's Pepper Pot, North African Vegetable, Autumn Gold Squash. Moosewood mothers me.

When I'm not having an all-vegetable kind of day, which is fairly regularly, I'm probably having a what-to-do-with-chicken-this-time kind of day. There are a million things to do with chicken, of course. And my Old Standby, Cheryl Sedaker, suggests 365 of them. *365 Ways to Cook Chicken* is as pragmatic and unpretentious as the title implies. Cheryl is not above dressing one's chicken bits in smushed-up corn-flakes. Or peanut sauce or mustard or ginger-spiked yogurt. She makes a fine chicken pot pie. And she doesn't fuss.

Elizabeth David doesn't fuss either. But you won't find Elizabeth, sensible and instructive as she is, in my armload of much-beloved Old Standbys. For one thing, she's very much attached to my husband, Chris. They're both Brits, that may have something to do with it: Chris is perfectly at home with gammon and marrow and "a half a teacup full of claret." He knows what "Heat an oven to Regulo 7" means. Not me. Cooking with Elizabeth David is a bit like reading Proust. I should. But I don't.

Then there's the cookbook that taught me how to cook, that's been at my side forever and always, the irreplaceable *Joy of Cooking*. Mine is the 1975 edition, the one with the red grosgrain bookmarks. Its spine is buckled and frayed; its cover a grimy montage of dribbles and splats from the hundred and one family dinners put together in its company. The pages crackle to the touch. Smeared notes in the margins give testimony to *Joy*'s infallible capacity to please: beside the recipe for Brownies Cockaigne on page 653— "*ooooh, yes!*"

Joy, more than any other cookbook, is like a beloved old auntie: wise, plainspoken, capable. She chats as we cook— about tamales, making biscuits and how to skin a squirrel. *Joy* knows exactly how long to boil the marmalade, how much to stir the muffin batter and precisely when the court bouillon is sufficiently atremble to immerse the fish.

And as for the eighty-odd malingerers on my shelf—well, I should really just pitch them out. Perhaps have a ceremonial burning for my nemesis, *China Moon.* But I know I never will. They're like a photo album, a record of my seriously chaotic life in the kitchen. And who knows? Maybe, one day, I *will* be eating rusks and counting calories and puzzling over what on earth to do with all that pig's liver in my fridge.

Pseudo Buco

This is in lieu of the genuine article, osso buco, a somewhat fussy, rather expensive Italian classic made with veal shanks. I use lamb shanks instead, an unforgivable breach of tradition, I know, but there you go. However, I have retained the essential component of any buco, osso or otherwise: the gremolada, a wondrously fragrant, citrusy concoction that's added to the slow-simmered stew at the very end.

4 lamb shanks
3 tablespoons butter
¼ cup olive oil
½ cup chopped onion
½ cup chopped celery
⅓ cup chopped carrots
2 cloves garlic, minced
¾ cup dry white wine
½ cup beef bouillon
1½ cups drained canned plum tomatoes, chopped
1 strip lemon peel
½ teaspoon dried thyme
Salt and pepper

Gremolada
2 tablespoons finely chopped parsley
1 clove garlic, minced
1 teaspoon grated lemon zest
1 anchovy fillet, finely chopped (You can leave this out if
  you're squeamish about anchovies.)

Preheat oven to 350°F.

Melt the butter with the oil in a sturdy, good-size casserole over medium-high heat, then brown the lamb shanks all over. Remove the shanks and set them to one side. Add the onions, celery, carrots and garlic to the pan and sauté until lightly browned. Return the lamb shanks to the pot, making sure the vegetables are well distributed around them. Add the wine, beef bouillon, tomatoes, lemon peel, thyme, a dash of salt and some freshly ground pepper. Bake, covered, until the meat is very tender (1½ to 2 hours), checking in halfway through to give it an encouraging stir.

Assemble the gremolada by mixing together the parsley, garlic, lemon zest and anchovy, if using. You can either stir this into the cooked pseudo buco 5 minutes before serving or pass it at the table for sprinkling. Pasta, lightly buttered, is an ideal accompaniment.

Serves 2 hungry people, 4 in a pinch.

If *Joy* is my kindly coach, Marcella Hazan is my commandant. In her books, getting it right is serious business. You don't mess around with Marcella. I learned this during a rigorous lesson on the dos and don'ts of assembling an authentic Italian ragù.

It was a bleak, rain-soaked November afternoon—a comfort-food day—and my heart cried out for pasta: pasta with a rich, slow-simmered Bolognese-style ragù. And because I'd noted that Marcella's recipe took a few curious turns, I was following directions slavishly.

This did not come easily. Usually, if a recipe fails to include the essentials of life—garlic or a splash of lemon juice or, at the very least, an excuse to use up that heel of red wine left over from the night before—I simply put things right.

This time I was in no position to argue. Marcella's instructions are spelled out in a clear, authoritative voice. She tells you precisely what is required and why. I admit to feeling slightly cowed. I felt I was being watched and would be dealt a sharp poke at the first sign of insubordination.

I feel the same when I'm cooking with Giuliano Bugialli. I do as I'm told. And it is Bugialli's ragù recipe I usually turn to when a hearty meat sauce is required. But I'm exploring the cuisine of a different region today, moving east, across the Apennines, from Bugialli's Tuscany to Bologna, in the "meat-and-fat-happy" region of Emilia-Romagna. This is how *The Atlantic Monthly*'s Corby Kummer describes the land of *parmigiana* and prosciutto, the area Hazan stoutly defends as the "richest gastronomic region in Italy." I had the queasy feeling I'd blundered into a war zone here and was determined to follow the rules of engagement to the letter.

Things didn't look promising. Garlic, for example, did not enter into the construction of this ragù. Nor did basil, parsley or oregano. Just a pinch of salt, a little fresh ground pepper and, of all things, nutmeg. Which is ridiculous, of course. You know that, I know that, but this is what we're up against. I was beginning to have serious doubts about Ms. Hazan's ability to distinguish a pasta sauce from a pudding.

Another red flag—there is no beef stock: just tomatoes, wine (white, I note glumly) and milk. I adjust my recipe-reading glasses and look again. Milk? That's what it says. Milk—a whole cupful. Ha-ha! This is hilarious! Does Marcella have a sense of humour? I think not. I think she's serious. I pour the now redundant red wine into a juice glass, toss it back and get to work.

The *battuto* comes first: chopped onions, carrots and celery. Sautéed in olive oil, my *battuto* becomes a *soffrito*. And, Marcella tells me, my *soffritto* must be *perfetto*: it is the foundation of flavours that will suffuse and define everything that follows. And what follows is the meat, with some salt and pepper, in a step known as *insaporire*.

Battuto. Soffritto. Insaporire. So far so good. But wait—here it comes. Oh no! The milk.

What I have now is a lumpy yellowish gruel with shimmering globules of fat cruising its surface. I search about for the dog but he is downwind of the proceedings and has prudently retired to his hiding place under the stairs. I'm on my own. Except for Marcella, of course, who insists I stir this grotesque porridge through its lugubrious burble and bubble until the milk, mercifully, at last disappears.

Nutmeg next—just a whisper because I'm convinced this too is folly. Then the wine (wrong colour) and the tomatoes (promising), after which the resultant sludge (pale pink) is left to sort itself out over three or four hours of slow cooking.

Marcella points out that a true Bolognese ragù is never served over spaghetti. Rigatoni, tagliatelle, fusilli, yes—but not spaghetti.

I cook spaghetti, relishing this small act of defiance, and add the ragù. It looks like something Ralston-Purina dreamed up for the pampered pet set. And it tastes . . . well, it tastes bloody wonderful. It tastes like the improbable miracle it is: rich and dense and subtly layered with flavours so exquisite we fall silent, marvelling at such goodness.

In tribute to Bologna, Marcella and tastes refined through time, I raise my glass and humbly eat my words.

The Problem with Parsley,
the Bugbear of Beets

My brief, unhappy fling with florentines put the lid on my seat-of-the-pants style of cooking. For a while at least. I now do pretty much as I'm told. Not always, but more often than not. I don't do as I'm told when there's room for debate, which there frequently is. Parsley and beets are, to my mind, subjects for debate.

I have deep reservations about parsley. James Beard insists on three parsley sprigs for a perfect beef bourguignon; *The Silver Palate*'s choucroute garni calls for four; Giuliano Bugialli's pommarola (tomato sauce) requires five.

Why parsley? Why this slavish sprig count? Why, in fact, bother at all? What does parsley bring to the table anyway? Cooking, shopping, life as we know it would be so much simpler without it. And, I suspect, a bourguignon just as good. The problem is, parsley doesn't come in sprigs. I never have just *three sprigs* of parsley. I either have no parsley at all when I need it or it's there, in banquet-size bunches, when I don't.

Unlike bay leaves or cloves or cardamom seeds, when you bring a bunch of parsley home *it* calls the shots. Just watch next time: the second you've extricated those few crucial sprigs for the soup kettle, the left-behinds instantly turn yellow, sink to their knees and die. No matter that they're standing, shin-deep, in a bath of life-saving water, they die. What is this? Separation anxiety? Spite? All I know is that they go down like ninepins, on cue, the moment your back is turned.

You could always "just say no" of course and avoid the bunch-purchase problem altogether. But I've not yet mustered the confidence required to breeze through a supermarket check-out with three sprigs of parsley in my cart.

"Will that be all for you today?"

"That's it."

"Will you be needing some help carrying that to your car?"

"You bet. I'll just make some room in the trunk."

(If you could buy tomato paste by the spoonful I'd do that too. Same rationale: you extract two spoonfuls from a twenty-spoonful can and grow green fur on the rest.)

There are four possible solutions to this supply-and-demand parsley conundrum: freeze it, dry it, grow it or forget it. I've tried them all and can recommend one. Frozen parsley tastes passably parsley-like, but in its splodgy reincarnation a career in the garnish department is ill advised. Dried parsley tastes of no parsley at all in my book. Growing it is fine for someone with a longer attention span and greener thumbs than mine. Besides, this is an extremely risky business. According to folklore and old witches' tales, the planting of parsley seeds will precipitate the instant death of someone near and dear. My advice? Forget it.

I'm not saying that parsley is good for nothing. It's just that I'm not sure it's worth all the angst. Besides, I don't think I could spot a parsley-enhanced lamb en daube from a parsley-deprived one. On the other hand, a tabouleh is not a tabouleh without parsley. In fact, in the handful quantities that so many Middle Eastern dishes call for, parsley is a taste sensation.

Another very good use for parsley is as a party-time accessory, a sort of personal garnish. The Romans used to wear garlands of it to their wine-soaked revels. They believed that it prevented the unpleasant effects of too much drinking. I've not tried this. But it could solve the two-birds-with-one-stone (hangover/leftover) problem.

Parsley is a pretty good breath freshener too, if garlic and onions are getting in the way of you and a good kiss. And it's loaded with iron and vitamin C. I read somewhere that, ounce for ounce, parsley provides as much vitamin C as an orange. This is good, I suppose, if you're prepared to snap on a feedbag and chomp your way through a bushel of the stuff.

But parsley is more than good nutrition. It's a reliable guide to the restaurant scene. Take note: if the parsley arrives in sprig form, next to the mash and alongside a curlicued orange slice, you're in good-value, family-dining heaven. If it comes tossed, confetti-like, over a highrise construct in a puddle of coulis, you're probably out of your depth and paying too much.

Parsley's been around practically forever so it shouldn't be dismissed out of hand. Besides, there are nuances that are probably worth exploring: the flat-leafed Italian variety is, I'm told, superior to the more familiar curly-leafed, family-restaurant favourite. I've not investigated these niceties. That would require bringing home *two* bunches of parsley, and doubling the death toll in my kitchen. No, I can live without parsley. And parsley, I assure you, can live without me.

I could not, however, live without beets. I love beets. I just hate dealing with them.

There's a kind of beet called mangelwurzel. It's orange, coarsely textured and is usually fed to cattle. The name means "root for time of need"—in other words, it's what you eat when the wolf's at the door and even the turnips are gone. Quite frankly, I think there's a stubborn little remnant of the mangelwurzel gene lurking in the whole *Beta vulgaris* family. A sort of built-in user deterrent that insures that no matter how hungry you are, the last thing you'll eat is a beet.

Aesthetics are partly to blame. There's nothing even remotely seductive about a beet. It has none of the priapic suggestiveness of asparagus. It's not nearly as cute as a baby pea. It lacks the sophistication of the artichoke. A beet is a lump of a thing with a rough, somewhat shabby skin that looks like it needs a good scrubbing. Which is out of the question, of course, because a scrubbed beet bleeds.

Beets bleed no matter what you do. You can't poke them and you certainly can't peel them because they'll hemorrhage during cooking and their intense colour and much of their taste will be lost. So you have to cook them in their skins and then, theoretically, if the beet is done just right—sheer guesswork because of the "no poking" rule—the skin will slide off obligingly under a stream of cold water. The thing is, it doesn't. Beets are notoriously reluctant to doff their skins. I also find that cold showers tend to produce cold beets. And a hot beet, like a hot potato, is a difficult thing to pin down.

In 1861 *Mrs. Beeton's Book of Household Management* offered this advice: "If the beets are to be served hot," it says, "rub off the peel quickly." Right. Have you ever tried massaging a hot beet? Or wielding a peeler with your hands encased in oven mitts?

But I persist, and have persisted for all these many years, because beets are so darn good. Borscht is beautiful. Beets—cold, hot, glazed, puréed, pickled or shredded in salads—are sublime. But nothing in the world can compare to the taste of a beet that's been baked, snugged in foil and left to fend for itself in a 325°F oven for about an hour and a half. The flavour—that incomparable, earthy-sweet beetiness—fills the mouth with an explosive rush that leaves everything that follows tasting like Wonder bread in comparison.

But a baked beet still requires peeling. You still have to shower it and shave it and get it to the plate. A taste sensation it may be, but the bloody thing still leaks.

According to Sheila Lukins and Julee Rosso in *The New Basics Cookbook,* there is a beet on the market now, a gold-fleshed variety, that doesn't bleed. I've never seen one. It could be a natural wonder. Or a genetic fiddle—another example of biotech wizardry brought to bear on the mangel-wurzel effect to stop the carnage. Anything is possible. After all, if they can jam a gene from a cold-water fish into strawberries to make them frost-resistant, a leak-proof beet should be a piece of cake.

As for the peeling problem . . . well, there's bound to be something in the genetic lending library for that too. What about tangerines? They shed their skins without much fuss. As do snakes.

One day, I'm sure, we'll be offered the choice: the flawed but familiar Heritage Classic that turns the mash pink and is virtually impossible to peel. Or a new, improved, zip-skin, leak-resistant model that goes from pot to plate with all the fuss-free efficiency of the boil-in-a-bag dinner it was designed to accessorize.

In the meantime—and despite the bother—let's hope that nature stays the course. And the beet goes on.

(This just in . . . some very good news for those of you with beet-blistered hands, parsley on your conscience and too many thumbs. I think you call this an editor's note.)

To peel a beet: simply spear the hot beet on the tines of a fork. Hold the forked beet in one hand and wield your peeler with the other.

To keep parsley fresh: wash it, dry it well, separate the leaves from the stems and store them in a jar or a sealed plastic bag in your fridge.

Life, in this kitchen at least, will never be the same.

Chocolate Beet Cake

You're going to have to take my word on this one. I did not make this up. I could not, in a million years, have dreamed up anything this eccentric. The recipe came from Lasqueti Island Annie, a fine cook and a dear friend. When I bake a cake, this is the cake I bake.

1¾ cups all-purpose flour
1½ cups white sugar
½ cup good-quality cocoa powder
1½ teaspoons baking soda
Dash of salt

3 eggs

1⅛ cups vegetable oil

1 teaspoon vanilla

1 ¼ cups mashed, cooked beets

Preheat oven to 350°F. Grease a 13- by 9-inch baking pan.

Sift into a large bowl the flour, sugar, cocoa, baking soda and salt. In another large bowl, whisk the eggs. Whisk in the oil, vanilla and beets. Add the dry ingredients and beat for 2 minutes. Pour batter into pan.

Bake cake for 30 minutes or until a toothpick inserted in its centre comes out clean. Cool in pan before removing.

And Another Thing: Fish

If beets and parsley had me stumped, fish takes the cake. I'm completely befuddled by fish. Not the cooking of—that's easy. Fish (good fish, wild and fresh and tasting robustly fish-like) needs little embellishment. A coating of lightly seasoned flour, a nub of butter, a sturdy cast-iron skillet are all that's required. But I do like to know what I'm eating. With fish you're never sure: they travel under assumed names.

"Most fish called bass are really something else," writes A. J. McClane in his comprehensive *Encyclopedia of Fish Cookery.* I would amend that observation: most fish, *no matter what they're called*, are almost certainly something else. One man's wahoo is another man's tinker. They're both mackerel. Or kingfish. You name it. And if you don't like the name you can change it. It happens all the time.

Dogfish is a classic example. Nobody wanted to eat battered dogfish, for heaven's sake, so this small shark species, often referred to as "trash fish" by commercial fishermen, proved to be a dismal failure in Britain's fish-and-chip shops. But it was plentiful and affordable and it tasted good, so the dogfish spin doctors called a meeting and decided the simplest thing to do was change the name. So dogfish became rock cod. It sold like hotcakes.

This kind of thing wouldn't be tolerated in any other food category. You can't go calling garbanzo beans jelly beans just to please a persnickety public. A Brussels sprout is very obviously a Brussels sprout, and changing its name isn't likely to persuade anybody otherwise.

Fish enjoy a lot more latitude. And we've encouraged it. We recoil at the sight of a fish head. We don't like to eat anything whose countenance is displeasing. Or whose name doesn't have a jolly culinary ring. So most of us wouldn't really know mullet from John Dory if we were pressed to make the distinction. We like our fish in neat breaded squares, or anonymous fillets, so a change of name in the interests of marketing pragmatics goes largely unnoticed.

But this confusing business of nomenclature isn't solely a product of marketing whimsy. Many of the common names given to the fish we eat reflect the history and tradition of the various regions of the world where they are found. For instance, in the northeastern United States, porgy is referred to as "scup," a name derived from the Narraganset Indian word *mishcuppauog*.

A. J. McClane acknowledges the bewildering discrepancies in fishy nomenclature. Fish, he concedes, "are often a mystery, not solely to the amateur chef but to the *garde-manger* of some of the world's best restaurants." Which is why I have taken it upon myself to sort things out. With McClane's vast store of knowledge at my elbow and *The Fish Book* by Kelly McCune close by, I have compiled, for the curious and completely at sea like me, this quick and easy guide to who's who in the fish world.

Starting with ahi. Not to be confused with mahi-mahi, a dolphinfish or dorado as it's sometimes called, ahi is the Hawaiian name for yellowfin tuna. Which is also called big-eye. Then there's sea bass, which is not a bass but a drum. Giant sea bass, which is sometimes called black sea bass, or jewfish, isn't a bass either. It's a grouper. Black sea bass, on the other hand, is indeed a bass. As is striped bass, which is sometimes called rockfish but isn't a rockfish at all. The Pacific red snapper *is* a rockfish but isn't even remotely related to the Atlantic red snapper, which is in fact a true snapper. Hake is related to the cod, as is the haddock, and a young cod is called a scrod. Canadian black cod isn't actually cod at all but sablefish, which is also called, perversely, Alaska cod. Sablefish is often referred to as butterfish as well, but isn't. Nor is white perch a perch. It's a bass. The ocean perch isn't actually a perch either. It's a rockfish. The orange roughy, sometimes called a slimehead, is, however, a perch. The walleyed pike is a perch as well and not a pike at all. Nor are yellow pike or blue pike actually pike—unlike the pickerel, which is, in fact, a small pike. Wolf fish sometimes masquerades as ocean catfish, which is doubly confusing as catfish is a freshwater fish with the exception of the catfish known as hogfish, which is a saltwater variety. Dolly

Varden trout and lake trout aren't actually trout but char. And Arctic char is a relative of both salmon and trout. Unlike Dover sole, which is a true sole, the sole we eat probably isn't sole at all but flounder, which is often marketed as turbot. The monkfish or goosefish, which tastes like shellfish because that's what it feeds on, is also known as angler fish. The sprat is a small herring, which when packed in oil is called brisling. And what is sometimes marketed as sea veal or sea bass or even sometimes greyfish is actually shark. Mullet was renamed lisa in the U.S. until people started asking "What the heck's a lisa?" and it went back to being a mullet. Which is what the Canadian government has chosen to call the sucker. And the sucker . . . well, I'll leave you to sort that one out for yourself.

I hope this helps.

The More the Messier

All things considered—mystery fish, bleeding beets and Windex-encrusted bread—the addled cook is well advised to abdicate responsibility to a willing kitchen crew whenever possible. You don't call them your "kitchen crew," of course. They're guests. They have been assigned a place of special honour in your kitchen: they're cooking dinner.

It's like a potluck supper really, except everything happens on the spot, freestyle—a sort of potluck run amuck. One such event is the Do-It-Yourself Cornish Hen Stuffathon.

The premise is simple: each guest is handed a Cornish hen and told to stuff it.

The first Stuffathon, involving four hens and four plucky hen handlers, was held on New Years's Day in 2000. It was mayhem. The kitchen took on all the high-intensity heat of a war room. A couple of contestants, unaccustomed to the niceties of stuffing birds, launched into some quite improbable combinations. One concept, involving corn chips, sun-dried tomatoes, green olives and pine nuts, was abandoned early on for obvious reasons and the bird in question was dispatched unceremoniously into the oven, stuffing free except for a single onion. It was disqualified.

In the end, three prizes were awarded, one for aesthetic appeal, one for originality and one for good taste.

The winner of the aesthetics prize was the guest who opted for simplicity: Paxo (the just-add-water stuffing-from-a-box) enhanced only with the discreet addition of sautéed onions and sage. I thought he should have been docked points for this dispirited effort, but, unlike the rest of us who found our attention wandering as the wine circulated, he bustled and basted and tended to his entry with exemplary care. In the end there was no question that his skillfully stuffed and trussed bird looked magnificent, like a centre-fold in *Saveur,* with its crispy golden skin, its little legs crossed primly at the ankles and absolutely no stuffing leakage that could be detected by the judge. This contestant got bonus points for making the communal gravy: silky smooth and Bisto-brown. (Bisto—essentially cornstarch, salt and caramel for colouring—also comes in a box. The perfect accompaniment to its idiot-proof meal-mate, Paxo.)

For originality, the prize went to the person who placed last in the aesthetics category. His bird burst apart in the oven, so overwhelmed was it with both the volume and the incongruity of the ingredients it had been forced to accommodate: chestnuts chopped into uneven lumps, to which were added wild rice, scraps of apricot fruit leather, cinnamon and generous lashings of cheap Spanish brandy. The contestant delivered enough chestnut-brandy stuffing into the bird's tiny cavity to fill a welterweight turkey. The finished piece, post-explosion, looked like the contents of our compost bucket. The perpetrator insisted that it tasted "brilliant." It was not, however, high on the list for the "trade-you-a-bit-of-yours-for-a-bit-of-mine" exchange.

The winner in the good taste category was me. The bird of the hour was stuffed as follows: wild rice, cooked until tender and tossed with slivers of porcini mushrooms, pine nuts, sliced roasted peppers, garlic and a jolt of sake. It was, according to the judge's notes, "exquisitely subtle and inventive, a sublime and tasteful marriage." Not everyone agreed. But, as I pointed out, the decision of the judge was final. I was the judge.

One final note: the soup we concocted from these eclectic remains tasted like nothing on earth. Brandy and sake, combined with the spicy-sweet overlay of cinnamon and chestnuts, proved inedible. We used it to dress up the dog's daily dish of kibble until he finally dug in his heels, all four of them, and embarked on a hunger strike.

A similarly chaotic do-it-yourself free-for-all can be arranged around pizza. Everybody is given their own personal pizza pan and a wad of dough. A selection of toppings—the more the messier—is passed around (along with the scotch bottle) and from here on in it's every chef for himself.

Admittedly, things don't always go smoothly, especially at the dough-shaping stage of the operation. Pizza dough tends to insinuate itself into odd configurations that bear no resemblance to the neat round one is aiming for. Rolling pins and counter space are usually at a premium and anyone attempting the overhead toss technique is usually disappointed. Especially in small kitchens with low ceilings. And there is a tendency among the inexperienced to overestimate the tonnage that one nine-inch round of pizza dough can accommodate. A self-cleaning oven is essential for this event.

The success of the do-it-yourself dinner party depends on your capacity to delegate. This is sometimes difficult as the temptation to intercede when you see a disaster in the making is enormous. Sardines and pineapple, for example, may not be your idea of correct pizza protocol, but the considerate host will avert her eyes and reserve comment.

What you'll find is that everyone takes immense pride in his or her own creation and guards it jealously from inception to table. There's a wonderful intimacy about cooking together and squabbling with one's neighbour over a pile of shredded mozzarella or a stash of olives. But the best part of the kitchen-crew concept is that you're off the hook and home free. For the accident prone, there's no safer place to be.

Chris's Own Cheese-free Pizza

This is Chris's signature pizza. It's what he creates, in his own quiet way in his own ordered space, amidst the pizza-building bedlam around him. It's called pissaladière, a traditional peasant-style dish from Provence that calls for nothing but onions, olive oil, black olives and anchovies. The secret lies in the long, slow cooking of the onions. And no cheese.

(I like to add a generous pinch of thyme and some garlic to the onions as they simmer. A travesty, some would say, and none of my business.)

¼ cup top-quality extra-virgin olive oil, plus a bit more to grease the pan
2 or more large onions (about 2 pounds in all), thinly sliced (Chris uses Walla Wallas)
½ to ¾ pound pizza dough, enough for a 10-inch pan (recipe follows)
10 to 12 pitted black olives (never, ever use canned!)
8 to 10 anchovies

Preheat oven, about an hour ahead of time, to 500°F. Grease a 10-inch pizza pan with a bit of the olive oil.

Over a medium-low burner, heat the rest of the oil in a large cast-iron skillet, one that has a cover. Add the onions, stir to coat thoroughly with the oil, and let them cook very, very slowly for about 45 minutes, stirring them from time to time. They're meant to melt, not brown, so you may want to cover them for the final 15 minutes or so.

When the onions are very soft, spread them on the pizza

dough that you've skillfully manipulated to fit the pan. Arrange the olives and anchovies on top. Bake for about 15 minutes or until the crust is golden.

Pizza dough

It's tempting to buy commercial ready-to-load pizza crusts because they're at-hand and easy. But if you can spare the time to make your own it's so much better. The problem with the do-it-yourself approach is that you must anticipate, at breakfast, an undeniable urge for pizza at dinnertime. I always know these things. You may have other matters on your mind while you're eating your cornflakes.

This recipe makes enough dough for four 10-inch pizzas.

1½ cups warm water
2½ teaspoons active dry yeast
½ teaspoon sugar
3½ cups all-purpose flour
1½ teaspoons salt

Put the warm water into a bowl, stir in the yeast and sugar, and let it sit for about 10 minutes until it's foamy. In the meantime, put the flour and salt in a food processor. Turn it on and, using the feed tube, slowly pour in the yeast mixture. Keep it whizzing until the dough wraps itself up into a ball. If you need more water add it judiciously, a tablespoon at a time. Don't worry if the dough is a bit sticky. That will correct itself in the pummelling that follows.

Turn out the dough onto a lightly floured surface. Give it a shove. Push it around. Lift it up and slam it down. Let it know who's boss. This is not puff pastry we're dealing with here: the firmer your hand, the better your dough will be. Keep up this roughhousing for 3 or 4 minutes, using a dough scraper if you meet with any resistance and adding flour only if all else fails. You should end up with a smooth, pliant ball of dough, which you may now oil lightly and place in a roomy, high-sided bowl. Cover it tightly with plastic wrap and let it sit at room temperature for the rest of the day—7 or 8 hours—or until it has tripled in bulk.

Now it's time to be gentle. No punching or shoving. With loving hands, remove your dough carefully from the bowl and slice it into 4 portions. You can freeze what you don't use. Or wrap each portion loosely in plastic wrap and keep it in the fridge for 3 to 4 days.

Coming of Age
Less-than-Gracefully

A word of caution: there's a world of difference between delegating and letting go. I can delegate, no problem. Delegating is simply a matter of managing the job so you don't have to do the work. But letting go is something else again. It means backing off, butting out, and trusting someone else to do what you thought couldn't possibly get done without you. You know you're grown up when you've learned to let go. Let go *gracefully*, that's the trick. And I'm not there yet, a fact that became painfully apparent on the occasion of my last birthday.

In honour of the day I was to be treated to an extra-special, once-a-year slap-up dinner. I was pretty confident that it would be exactly as billed because I happen to be on fairly intimate terms with the chef-in-residence. I've seen what miracles can be wrought with a few lumps of frozen goat meat and a can of Patak's curry.

I've heard it said that there is no sight on earth more moving than that of a beautiful woman in the act of preparing a meal for the man she loves. I disagree. I think the most heartwarming sight in the world is that of a beautiful man cooking dinner for the woman he loves. Much of the appeal of this turn-about scenario is of course its rarity. Lots of men like to cook. But too few possess either the confidence or the inclination to commandeer the kitchen in the name of love. An armful of roses is a whole lot easier to cobble together than a pepper-dusted rib roast with cèpe marmalade. Besides, some women can't bear to pass by a bubbling pot without nosing in and passing comment. You know women like that. My personal chef certainly does.

The meal was to remain a secret until the moment of presentation. I am used to secrets. The chef is renowned for his caginess. He's kept his Colonel Chris's Island Fried Chicken recipe under wraps for years. He says it's in the hands of his lawyers and will be released over his dead body.

I love surprises. But secrets drive me crazy. That you can't have one without the other is a leap of logic that has so far eluded me. So I pry.

"If it's scallops"—I toss this out casually—"you know, if scallops were even a remote possibility, which maybe they are and maybe they aren't—you don't have to say—but say they were and you needed a recipe . . ."

The chef is noncommittal on the subject of scallops.

"On the other hand, if you're thinking beef, a nice little rib-eye perhaps . . ." (Hard to tell if he's thinking beef.) "Or there's a clever Cajun thing you could do with snapper." Poke, prod, wheedle, wheedle. I stop short of peeking into the tiny parcels and tubs that are beginning to accumulate on the No Trespassing shelf in the fridge.

The chef—oh dear, is he feeling harassed?—takes pity.

"Each day for the next three days," he says, "one essential ingredient will be revealed. Just one. You may extrapolate from the clues what you will." Oh, goodie!

On Day One of the countdown he unveils the wine: a Georges Dubœuf Beaujolais Nouveau. Smashing! I smack my lips and make a dive for the corkscrew. Ha-ha. Just teasing! What a wag I am!

Day Two reveals a teensy-weensy carton of—*gasp!*—whipping cream! Glory be! I check the butterfat content (33%) and lie in wait.

Birthday day. The chef produces clue No. 3: a mushroom.

"Ooh!" I sigh. "Mushrooms on toast! No. Wait—let's weigh the evidence. *Creamed* mushrooms on toast. That's it! With a tumbler of Beaujolais on the side."

But the chef, in consultation now with Alain Ducasse,

Elizabeth David and other event organizers, is unavailable for comment.

Preparations are under way in earnest by early afternoon. My instructions are to curl up by the fire with a good dog and generally make myself scarce. This is patently impossible of course, what with all the *sizzle-sizzle-whisk-chop* sounds and warm buttery smells I can't quite identify that lure me inexorably kitchenward. I prowl, sniffing the air, just outside the no-go zone. Just in case I'm needed.

"Can I get you anything?" I offer. "Bouquet garni? A splash of brandy? Truffle dust?"

The chef assures me everything is well in hand.

"Well . . . if the guinea fowl needs plucking . . ."

I am handed a generous birthday scotch, a semi-solved crossword puzzle and the suggestion that all the help required at the moment thank-you-very-much is with 7-down. By now, it was beginning to occur to me that with the impressive number of birthdays I have to my credit I could, quite legitimately, if I put my mind to it, consider myself a grown-up and start behaving like one. Right you are. I polish off my scotch and wait, with infinite grace, for dinner to be served.

Here is the gift that came my way: Belgian endive with cracked walnuts and a crumbly Roquefort cheese lightly bathed with a lemony vinaigrette. Next: a lavishly pampered twelve-step multi-saucepan blanquette de veau à l'ancienne avec—Ooh-la-la!—sauce velouté de button mushrooms and pearl onions. This was served with baby carrots, red-skinned potatoes and beaucoup de frisky Beaujolais. The finale: one perfect red Bartlett pear and an Explorateur triple-cream cheese with crackers.

Exquisite.

Reality Check

Nobody bats a thousand every time they step up to the stove. Some of us don't even come close. And on an average day in your average kitchen, mess happens. Except on TV. It's amazing how seamlessly life unfolds on TV.

I am watching Emeril Lagasse make a seafood chowder. Emeril is a TV chef. His stage is a shiny TV kitchen with lots of shiny pots and pans and his own in-house band. The band provides the musical flourishes—a drum roll here, a riff there—to accompany Emeril's culinary ones. The camera moves in lovingly for the dicing of the celery. The studio audience looks on, transfixed, as if they were witnessing the laying on of hands.

I'm thinking, wait a second—*wait a second!* The guy's just making *soup*. Why am I here?

I chop celery. *You* chop celery. We all chop celery. So it's not the glamour of the process that holds us in thrall. We don't gather round the television for vacuuming demonstrations or to watch laundry being folded. But we're putty in the hands of TV cooks doing everyday things in make-believe kitchens. It's most peculiar.

It's not as if we're likely to witness some unexpected domestic catastrophe, like a soufflé imploding or a jam that won't gel. Mistakes came with the territory in the oopsy-daisy, warts-and-all world that Julia Child inhabited. Not anymore. In today's TV kitchens nothing goes awry because cooks get to rehearse every meal before they make it for real. And wouldn't *that* be a treat! If I were going to whip up an expensive and complicated cassoulet, for example, I'd leap at the chance to muck around till I got it right, have someone clean up after me, then do it all over again. For large sums of money. The television cooking show is a slice of culinary life as we wish it could be: no one burns the toast or gets tangled up in a garlic braid on TV.

You wouldn't catch Emeril or Nigella dithering over a lump of frozen stewing beef and wondering *now what?* No dreaming and drooling over a stack of cookbooks while you ponder your options and the icy brick-that-will-be-dinner dismantles itself in the microwave. No wine splashed into a tumbler to amuse you while you wait. In TV land the beef comes pre-cubed and camera-ready. The garlic's minced, the onion's sliced, and our super-chef just happens to have lemongrass and juniper berries and five-spice powder all miraculously at hand in tidy, pre-measured piles. None of this rummaging through jumbled drawers while the onions frizzle to black and the rice boils over.

And where is the cookbook, for heaven's sake? How can you cook without a book propped open in front of you, your place secured under the weight of the ketchup bottle and your reading glasses clouded with flour?

Another thing: did you ever notice that there are no phones

in this never-never land? Our aproned hero won't get caught with a cabbage in one hand and the phone in the other explaining why this is really not the optimum moment to discuss monthly donations to the Save-the-Marmot fund.

And where is the cat? Why is there no cat sliding around our chef's ankles and mewling for his ration of salmon skin? No dog either, to bump a cold nose against an elbow till the butcher wrap, slick with meat juice, is delivered.

You'll notice too that TV cooks are always impeccably turned out, as if the moment all this pesky domestic business is behind them they'll be off to the Ritz for tea. How do they do that? Do they never splatter tamari down a shirt front? Or dunk their cuffs in egg yolk? I suspect they even wear shoes.

I think we have to dig deep and travel far back to the earliest chapters of history to fully appreciate the phenomenon of the TV cooking show. There's something at work here that's as ancient as the stars and as irresistible as gravity, and I think it all started way back whenever, with the first bonfire.

In those long-distant pre-Emeril days, cooking was pretty much a catch-as-catch-can affair. The menu depended entirely upon what the earth yielded up or what four-legged main course wandered by. So you couldn't just snap your fingers, decide that what you really fancied right about now was a nice bouillabaisse and shop accordingly. Your kitchen was where you built your fire. And if you needed a pot you found some clay and made one. Food was precious. A blessing. Collecting it, preparing it, cooking it was a communal effort, and hard work.

Picture a cozy row of cave houses somewhere in the dusty hills of ancient Khuzistan. Little cave-kids crouch in the firelight playing pick-up-sticks with bison bones. The women folk, fetchingly decked out in hyena-hide aprons, take turns over a bubbling pot of knobbly roots and wild greens.

"Let's hope the boys get back while the fire's hot," they say. "Let's hope they bring home the bacon."

They do—they've bagged a boar—and they emerge through the gloaming to a hero's welcome, dragging their dinner behind them. Chunks of flesh are torn from the great beast and flung into the fire. As the meat sizzles and the air fills with the promise of feasting to come, the children abandon their games and join the company around the fire. Food brings them together, in gratitude and awe, to drink in the dazzle of man's first cooking show.

Fast-forward if you will and look how far, in leaps and bounds, we've come since then! Our chops come pre-apportioned in cello-wrapped six-packs; we no longer mash our turnip with a rock; our greens, pre-washed, know no seasons; and we can switch our cook fires off and on at will. But the true measure of how far we've come, and what we've left behind, is here, in a made-for-TV kitchen where we've gathered to watch soup being assembled to music.

We've made great strides, all right. But I've got a hunch we've rather overshot.

4

Tomorrow
We May Diet

Whenever I think about dieting
I lie down till the feeling passes.

MIMI FURST

Weighing In

From time to time I toy with the notion of one day, maybe, going on a diet. Happily, common sense generally prevails. There are so many good reasons *not* to diet: chocolate, grilled cheese sandwiches, salty frites. And butter. The concept of life without butter—a piece of *toast* without butter—triggers a panic attack.

It's not that I haven't tried dieting. I have. But it's not gone well. I get cranky, I feel gypped. I cheat. Cheating begets guilt which begets anxiety which usually begets a comforting splodge of peanut butter on a hunk of homemade bread.

I eat far more sensibly when I'm *not* dieting. After all, on any given day I am surrounded on all sides by good food. Arriving home with the bounty from my friend's market garden is a cause for rejoicing. A plate of steamed chard is all the happiness I need. Until I'm told it's all the happiness I'm allowed. Which is what happens on an annual basis every time I check in with my doctor.

The Weigh-In is the worst part. I step on the scales and exhale mightily in a pathetic effort to lighten the load. The assistant with the clipboard sighs and records the kilos.

"It's the rain," I say. "I'm waterlogged."

I am ushered to a cubicle where I don a paper dressing gown and sit on a paper sheet to prepare myself for the Interrogation.

On my last visit my doctor had announced that I was stockpiling what appeared to be large lumps of Crisco in my veins. There are two kinds of cholesterol, she informed me: the good stuff, and the bad stuff. I was up a quart on both counts. That's when she issued my diet guidelines. There were two lists: *Foods to Use* and *Foods to Avoid.* The latter being a complete catalogue of every ingredient essential to a full and happy life: mascarpone, croissants, gravy, Miss Vickie's potato chips. And butter of course. Beef tallow was also on the list but that was okay as I wasn't altogether sure what beef tallow was. My doctor explained: it's animal fat. Damn.

There were two notable non-mentions that I seized upon instantly. Pizza, for example, had somehow been overlooked in this joyless litany of dos and don'ts. And, to my delight, even alcohol had been given grudging approval by the party poopers from Calorie Control. Alcohol, with a prim reminder of the virtues of moderation. I'm fine with that. I've always assigned fairly liberal parameters to the concept of moderation.

I lost no time in consulting other experts in the field. I have lots of books on the subject. My idea of dieting is to read about it voraciously.

The vegetarian route comes highly recommended, and I grazed briefly here. Soybeans, radish sprouts, tofu . . . why not? But then my eyes fell upon an oddity: cottonseed, one of the richer sources of vital protein in a meatless diet. The

116

notion of sitting down to a bowl of cottonseeds gave me pause. I turned for solace to Adelle Davis, nutritionist and author of *Let's Get Well* and *Let's Eat Right to Keep Fit*. She's dead, I know. People keep pointing this out to me. Jack Kerouac is dead too. That doesn't cancel his road trip.

Adelle Davis was a pioneer, and a woman after my own heart. She maintained that the only surefire way to lower cholesterol is to consume it in vast quantities. In fact, if you were a laboratory monkey the recommended regimen would involve the injection of pure uncut cholesterol directly into the bloodstream. This would signal the liver (Cholesterol Production Headquarters) that the required quota of bacon grease and triple-cream cheese had been delivered. The liver, on being informed of this infusion of manna, would immediately cease production and—presto! A cholesterol overrun becomes a cholesterol deficit.

This is a radically simplified version of Davis's theory, I must confess. But she does cite a native tribe in Africa that derives 65 percent of its calories from butterfat. They eventually die, of course. But they go with grease on their chins and a good meal in their bellies and not from heart disease. Inspired, I revise my doomsday list. Things are looking up. Beef tallow is in. Butter is back. And pizza's looking good. I have a glass of wine to celebrate.

My doctor couldn't grasp the logic of this at all. No, she said, the exclusion of pizza from the list did not give me carte blanche to chow down at will. And alcohol, even in trace amounts, was not a recommended substitute for carrot juice.

"So you like a drink," she said, stating the obvious.

"Oh yes!" I said.

"*What* do you drink?"

"Well, I quite enjoy a nice gin and tonic. Negronis are good. But mostly I drink wine."

"How much?"

"Half a bottle."

"Half a *bottle?* Every *day?*" She looked genuinely horrified.

"We have a bottle of wine with dinner. Between us. And we have dinner once a day," I explained.

This was the wrong answer. She fixed me with her let's-work-this-out-together-shall-we look and asked if I considered my *habit* to be a *problem*.

No, I assured her. The only *problem* was when we ran out. When we were forced to dip into our vat of homemade blackberry plonk, which, because of its unique vinaigrette-like bite, we often sloshed on salads as well. I congratulated myself on having introduced salads to the discussion.

I didn't get the Lecture. Just the Look. We then moved on to a full and frank discussion of my obvious penchant for all of life's most desirable and frowned-upon things. This encounter took place several years ago now and I've been living happily with my "problem" ever since.

I'd tactfully avoided raising the subject of Hippocrates, author of the oath and father of modern medicine. I think that was wise. She'd not suggested I seek a second opinion. But it is worth noting that Hippocrates was very much in favour of wine. He relied on it to treat all manner of ills. It cooled fevers, promoted digestion, nourished the convalescent and was widely used as an antiseptic. More to the point, Hippocrates himself, undoubtedly partial to the taste of his own medicine, lived to be nearly one hundred.

But that was two thousand years ago. My doctor is a modern doctor. And ours is a culture in which, for many, abstinence is a virtue. We embrace it with eagerness, as Margaret Visser points out, so that we may "sanctimoniously refrain."

Not me. And I'm in good company on that score. Take Robert Louis Stevenson. He called wine "bottled poetry." André Simon praised it as a multifaceted "work of art." Louis Pasteur declared it the "most healthful" of beverages. But my favourite take on the subject comes from C. J. Bayliss: "A meal without wine is—half a grapefruit and a bowl of Special K."

Wine, like bread and pottery, has been with us since the year dot. It's been a source of comfort, courage, healing, nourishment, inspiration, passion and pleasure for millennia. And because it enhances the food we eat and surely but gently releases us from the chains of our inhibitions, it was long ago recognized as the drink that, as Hugh Johnson put it in *Vintage: The Story of Wine,* "brought strangers together in high spirits and with open minds."

And it doesn't take much—which is, of course, the point. An Athenian statesman named Eubulus defined moderation with a very simple formula: pour one glass to your health. Pour a second to love and pleasure. And a third to sleep. More than this, he cautioned, would lead to uproar and drunken revel and biliousness. And that, the good doctor Hippocrates would tell you, is a problem.

The Classic Negroni

This is an elegant—and very potent—drink. One, in my experience, is quite enough. You may not agree. In which case I refer you to the in-depth discussion of morning-after remedies on pages 212–215.

2 ounces gin
1 ounce sweet vermouth
1 ounce Campari
1 slice orange

Pour the booze over ice cubes, stir well and garnish with the orange slice.

Eat like a Mouse

I don't track carbs or record calories. I refuse to count my peas or weigh my fish before I steam it. And who wants steamed fish anyway when you can have it sizzled in butter with a generous dollop of aïoli on the side? I've yet to succumb to the Atkins punishment plan. Or visit the Zone. There's even something called the Paleolithic diet that involves such time-honoured treats as pemmican, berries and leaves. I've not tried this either.

But never mind. All this nonsense may soon be behind us. Everything hangs on the fate of two roly-poly mice from Texas.

The story broke in *The Globe and Mail*. The headline, "Soon You Could Eat All You Like," was the answer to every failed dieter's dreams. There was a photograph of two mice side by side: bright button eyes, pink feet, fur the colour of cinnamon. They could have been identical twins except that the mouse on the left was a whole lot fatter than the mouse on the right. These mice, who live in a lab in Houston, have been on a diet—an all-you-can-eat diet, which, of course, is the regimen I've been espousing, in one guise or another, for years.

The mice have been pigging out for some time now, helping themselves to whatever's on offer whenever the mood strikes. Life's been good. The mice are happy. But the mouse on the right is going to be happy for a whole lot longer than his pudgy little pal on the left. He's had a gene-adjustment makeover.

By deactivating a certain gene, the body suppresses production of the enzyme acetyl-CoA carboxylase 2. It's called ACC2 for short and without it the body tends to burn fat off rather than pack it on. The svelte little rodent with his ACC2 button switched off has been eating like a horse. And the fat just melts away.

This metabolic wizardry is the handiwork of researchers at Baylor College of Medicine, in Houston. They are dedicated to the premise that people should be allowed to eat themselves silly and shed pounds while they're at it. However, a little dark cloud hangs over this Alice-in-Wonderland scenario. The more fat it has to burn, the harder a body has to work; the harder it works the hotter it gets; and the greater the heat generated the more likely it is that things could catch fire.

So. There's that to think about. It's one thing to slump down in a squashy chair with a bucket of fried chicken knowing that when you heave yourself up a few hours later you'll be twelve pounds lighter. It's quite another to eat yourself into a raging inferno and be reduced to a pile of ashes.

Another caution that has been raised is that there is a similar and related enzyme to ACC2. It's called ACC1. If they zap the wrong ACC button, you die. This too could take the fun out of dieting.

But assuming all the experiments go off without a hitch and this new pig-out, slim-down fiddle comes our way, what then? Can you imagine? The entire multi-million-dollar dieting industry would implode. Forget the carrot sticks. To hell with the carbs! We could sit around eating Twinkies and watching the Food Channel without a care in the world.

I raise a glass to those mice-with-a-mission in Texas. I wish them well.

Oh-So-Healthy Wilted Kale Salad

If you thought you didn't like kale, think again. This is so good. Not only that, it's like sitting down to a bowlful of megavitamins, and what could be more virtuous than that?

1 large bunch kale (about 16 leaves)
1 tablespoon balsamic vinegar
Salt and pepper
6 tablespoons extra-virgin olive oil
1 handful hazelnuts (a dozen or so), roughly chopped

With a sharp knife cut each kale leaf from its woody central stem. Chop the leaves as finely as you can and put them in a bowl. Sprinkle on the vinegar, add salt to taste, a generous grinding of black pepper, and toss until well combined.

Heat the oil in a small pan over medium heat and add the chopped hazelnuts. Let them sizzle, stirring gently, until they're slightly brown. Immediately pour the hot oil and nuts over the kale leaves and toss well as the kale wilts.

Serves 2.

Fat: How to Pack It On and Keep It On

It's a dodgy business, thinness. It's also a dreadful bore to anyone, like me, who has devoted a lifetime to the pleasures of the table. And for those of us who lean in ever widening circles toward rotundity, Brillat-Savarin's words—"Thinness is a horrible calamity for women"—ring with the seductive promise of a dinner bell. He goes on to say that because female beauty "consists above all of the roundness of their forms . . . every thin woman wants to grow plump."

How's that for a refreshing take on things? I envision myself trussed up like a Christmas goose and stuffed into yards of beaded brocade and hip-enhancing bustles, the envy of all the ladies at the ball.

Thinness, according to Brillat-Savarin, is not a problem for men. "They are no less vigorous for it, and are much more active." He supports this point with a reference to a male acquaintance who, though sparely built, "was strong enough to pick up with his teeth a heavy chair and throw it behind him by lifting it over the top of his head." Neat trick.

Brillat-Savarin devoted an entire chapter to correcting the problem of flesh-deficiency in women. Women are, he asserts, "no more difficult to fatten than young hens." After all, "we fatten sheep, calves, oxen, poultry, carp, crayfish and oysters." Why not women? Why not, indeed. The whole secret to acquiring plumpness, according to the

Brillat-Savarin manifesto, is to eat frequently and with due diligence. Here are some of the rules you must follow.

Eat plenty of bread. Fresh-baked is best. (No mention of butter here, but maybe that goes without saying.)

Breakfast before 8 A.M., preferably in bed. A cup of good chocolate will do. Or a bowl of soup thickened, again, with bread.

At 11 A.M. a hearty snack is recommended: fresh eggs, scrambled or fried in butter, and accompanied by meat patties or chops. (Veal? Pork? It's six of one, half a dozen of the other, I suppose. As long as the patty's fatty.)

A little exercise will help sharpen the appetite for the main meal to come. Brillat-Savarin has several suggestions, none of which, I'm happy to report, are terribly rigorous: a visit to your dressmaker; a brisk hop-skip-and-jump round the corner to the milliner's; a quick cruise-by of the fashion shops; then, with that little flurry behind you, you should call on your friends for cakes and tea and some happy chat about what you have seen.

Dinner: soup, meat, fish, macaroni, rice dishes, sweet custards, pastry and puddings.

There's more: Savoy biscuits, rum babas or anything made of flour, eggs and sugar. Beer too, and plenty of it, is highly recommended. If you're out of beer, wines (from Bordeaux or the Midi) will serve.

You must eat plenty of grapes. We're not told why. Make sure your baths are not too cool. Sleep a little or a lot, it doesn't matter, you'll pack on the pounds either way. If you sleep long, it is fattening. If you don't, you will digest your food that much more efficiently and be ready for a refill.

One final note: take care not to wear yourself out with too much dancing.

Brillat-Savarin promises that by following this regimen "with care and determination you will soon repair the ravages of nature." Nature has been abundantly kind to me, of course. But I do like the program. Perhaps I'll give it some thought—over a bit of bread and honey, in a not-too-cool bath, after I've visited my milliner.

A Table for One

When nobody's watching I melt cheese. I load it on whatever edible surface presents itself: from pizza, pasta and tuna-on-a-bun to corn chips and garlic-enhanced toast. I do not behave like this when Chris is in the house. This is my home-alone indulgence. And as M. F. K. Fisher so astutely observed, "Almost every person has something secret he likes to eat."

I have a theory about this. It's based mostly on hunch and partly on evidence gathered by prying into the private lives of friends and family. What I concluded was this: how we treat ourselves in solitude reveals more than any public performance ever could. And it's not what we eat so much as the measure of pleasure we squeeze from the moment.

For some, the home-alone occasion is a fine blend of unabashed hedonism and invention. For others it is a bleak hollow space in the day to be traversed with as much dignity as one can muster. You can slump down with a can of salmon in one hand and a spoon in the other. Or you may putter with happy purpose in the kitchen, a glass of wine within sipping reach and good smells all around.

Some people, when left to their own devices, slip into the comfort zone of their remembered childhood, re-creating the tastes and mealtime routines that nourished them in years gone by. These rituals, I discovered, frequently involve toast. Baked beans on toast. Canned spaghetti on toast. Sardines on toast. Stuff in general on toast. One improbable arrangement involves the boiling of a ripe tomato until the skin pops. It is then delivered to a slice of generously buttered, toasted white bread—white, no substitutes—then mushed to a soggy pulp with a fork and sprinkled all over with white pepper.

"Why white pepper?" I inquired.

"Because you have to see it," I was told.

One extraordinary creation, favoured by an otherwise sensible young woman, calls not for toast but for graham crackers. A handful or two are crumbled into a large cereal bowl, cold homogenized milk (it must be cold and it must be homogenized) is poured over top and the whole lot is smashed up into a sort of lumpy gruel. It's not for everyone. It's just for her.

Many, like me, seize upon solitude as a chance to eat what would never be countenanced, let alone shared, by their partner. I have a friend who has adopted a decidedly aggressive stance to this end. He has cordoned off one half of one shelf in the family refrigerator and stocked it with his personal home-alone provisions: German sausages, garlicky dills, pickled herring and black rye bread.

Then there's the home-alone-with-peanut-butter crowd. This is an essentially lazy bunch of loners as their inventions consist for the most part of hastily assembled sandwiches. My inquiries elicited a litany of variations on a recurring theme: peanut butter and Welch's grape jelly; peanut butter and banana; peanut butter, cucumber and sesame seeds; peanut butter and tomato; peanut butter, lettuce, mayo and bacon; peanut butter with a combination of any or all of the above.

One sandwich enthusiast, a Brit, mused dreamily on the delights of the chip butty: greasy fries scrunched between two pieces of buttered white bread.

Then of course there's the conscientious super-achiever who has chosen to live alone and is jolly good at it. He does laundry on Monday, irons on Tuesday and can be found any day of the week sitting down to a Health Canada–approved meal of meat or fish, one starch and two veg. (This category, I must point out, is based on conjecture only. I didn't actually encounter anyone of this persuasion.)

Sadly, many people live alone by dint of circumstances they would give the world to alter if they could. For them the home-alone routine is a dreary prospect indeed. It's like clipping your toenails, one woman said. Not much fun but it's got to be done. She showed me a typical meal, a package of something shrivelled and unrecognizable that would reconstitute itself in the microwave and emerge as a Salisbury steak. Never mind. It was food. It was good enough. It was just her, after all.

Which brings me to the lesson of Lucullus. Lucius Licinius Lucullus was a Roman general who retired in opulent style and became famous for his extravagant banquets and his generosity as a host. One day, grown weary of the company of others, he ordered his kitchen staff to prepare dinner for one.

It seems that Lucullus detected a certain dissonance in the palette of flavours set before him. Perhaps the wine was a degree or two too cold. Or too warm. Perhaps the sea urchins were too salty. Or the onion sauce that bathed the fallow deer was somehow lacking in lustre. When confronted, his chef admitted that as his lordship was dining alone it seemed somewhat unnecessary to fuss as one might have done had there been a lavish banquet to prepare.

To which Lucullus responded: "It is precisely when I am alone that you are required to pay special attention to the dinner. At such times, you must remember, Lucullus dines with Lucullus."

And you dine with you. Amen.

5

Yuck!
That's Offal!

*The thought of some poor ox flailing
around in search of his missing tail
kind of puts me off my stew.*

ALICE K. WITHERSPOON

Hold Your Tongue

What you see is what you get. Fair enough. The thing is, I knew perfectly well what I'd got, I just didn't like what I saw. Lolling there, mute and lumpish and disconcertingly out of context, was a very large grey tongue.

I was, inexplicably, quite unprepared for the fact that a tongue should look so, well . . . tongue-like. I'm not averse to tongues in general, being very much attached to my own. Tongues are extremely useful. They are covered with tiny taste buds to help you sort out what's good—like mangoes and lobster and single-malt scotch—and what's not. Raw sea urchin, for example. You need your tongue to distinguish a Merlot from a Cabernet and to swallow it without drooling. Tongues are good for exploring craters in molars and for ferreting out bits of peanut brittle from hard-to-reach crevices. Tongues are fine. In their place. And that place, I was beginning to suspect, was not at my table.

I'd bought it because it was there. Because, on your average day in your average supermarket, it rarely is. I was curious. I'd eaten tongue and enjoyed the experience but I'd never cooked one. Besides, it had looked innocuous enough amongst all the other shrink-wrapped bits and pieces—thighs, livers, oxtails, rumps—and I thought, why not?

The girl at the check-out broached it with caution, prodding it quickly through the scanner to the boy with the bags.

"What are you going to *do* with it?" she asked.

"I'm not entirely sure," I said.

If tongue looked like hamburger or a neat slice of sole it would be into the frying pan and onto the plate in a flash. But there was no disguising the fact that this dingy lump with its sandpaper roof was a tongue. A tongue just like mine. Only more so.

Liver presents no problem. I've never seen my own liver. I feel no queasy stab of recognition when I meet a chicken's gizzard. Or a cod's cheek. Even kidneys are sufficiently removed from the familiar to be manageable.

There are, I know, places in the world where the rat population is creatively culled by taking them off the streets and into the stew pot. I also appreciate the value of an open mind and an educated palate. On balance, I decided, I was lucky to have a tongue in my kitchen and not a rat. Now all I had to do was cook it.

Fortunately, I found the guidance I needed from the master of the art, Calvin Schwabe, in his appropriately titled study, *Unmentionable Cuisine*.

The first step was easy. I soaked it, for about three hours. I delivered it to the cooking pot (with some onion, celery, carrot and a bay leaf) and let it simmer away for another three hours. So far so good. The tricky bit was peeling the skin off the cooled tongue afterwards. It was easy to do, like peeling an orange. But I was unhappy doing it. It's hard to explain. I think it was the intimacy of it all that was so disconcerting.

This was a tongue that had lapped up puddle water, tasted spring grass. The thought very nearly stopped me in my tracks.

It tasted really good, lean and tender and delicately flavoured. There was, however, rather a lot of it. I needed a creative serving suggestion for several lunches' worth of cold boiled tongue. So once again I took my cue from Calvin Schwabe.

This pâté-cum-spread will come in specially handy if you encounter widespread resistance to the naked, in-your-face tongue presentation. It's good on little squares of dark rye bread or with thinly sliced cucumber in a sandwich. Its particular appeal lies in the fact that nobody will know it's tongue. I certainly see no need to bleat out your secret to all and sundry—*Can I pass you a little more macerated offal for that stack of naked crackers on your plate?* No, just pass the bowl and bite your tongue.

Pam's Offal Secret Pâté

¼ cup chopped hazelnuts

1 cup chopped cooked tongue

1 green onion, finely chopped

6 to 8 good black olives, pitted and chopped

1 large clove garlic, minced

½ teaspoon horseradish

Salt and pepper

3 tablespoons mayonnaise

Preheat oven to 300°F.

Place the hazelnuts in a small baking pan and toast them lightly in the oven for 7 to 8 minutes. Set aside to cool.

In your food processor, whiz up the nuts, tongue, green onion, olives, garlic, horseradish, salt and pepper until coarsely combined—avoid mushy. Put the mixture in a bowl, stir in the mayo and serve with head held high, as if it were an elegant pâté de foie gras.

Offal, in my book, refers to all things described as edible that I've decided aren't. Like tapioca. Coconut cream pie. And head cheese, which, of course, isn't cheese at all. Called "brawn" in Britain, head cheese is bits and pieces from a calf's head, or a pig's, that have been entombed in gelatin. This is truly offal in every sense of the word since it also happens to fit the official definition of the term: a variety of relatively obscure, generally-regarded-as-suspicious animal parts that, literally, "off fall" from a carcass when it is butchered. Stuff like brains, hearts, kidneys, liver, tripe and, as the Australian writer Terry Durack discovered, other unexpected tidbits that turn up from time to time.

Writing in Britain's *Independent on Sunday,* Durack recalled an occasion in a Japanese restaurant when a beaming restaurateur presented him with the house special: a delicate fish broth in which floated an enormous fish head. Durack slurped back the broth, which he pronounced superb. He then picked up his chopsticks and, with a few half-hearted stabs at the head itself, managed to snare a sliver of flesh from the tender cheek. Whereupon he sat back, sated and grateful, only to discover his host hovering anxiously nearby.

"But you've left the best bits!" he protested.

The best bits, it turned out, were the eyes.

"They taste just like oysters," his host insisted. "Only better."

Bravely, Durack broached the head, secured an eye and, navigating skillfully around a stiff upper lip, brought it to his mouth. It did indeed taste just like an oyster. Only better.

We don't like to eat eyes. We don't even want eye contact with eyes, not if they're staring back at us from a dinner plate. So fish heads are out. Boar's head is out. In fact any head, or any part of any head is, if not out, decidedly suspect. We don't like ears. Or snouts. Or brains. And some of us harbour serious doubts, still, about tongue.

Is it the taste of these bits and pieces that we find disagreeable? In some cases maybe, but, in North America at any rate, we're just as likely to refuse to try them at all. They're simply all-too-uncomfortable reminders that what we're eating actually had a life before we ended it. Besides, offal bits are often the bits that tend to slither and wobble. We don't like slither-and-wobble in our food. Except for Jell-O, of course. That's safe because that's just play food, brought to us by folks we can trust—the wonderful wizards at Kraft.

We eat lamb but we shy away from the likes of goat, donkey and mule. In many European cultures pig's ears and trotters are considered a treat. In Peking, duck's feet are deboned and tossed into salads. And in Greece it is an honour to be served the head of a spit-roasted lamb, complete with tongue and brains. The reality is that one man's "best bit" is another man's garbage.

Worms, for example. I don't eat worms but some people do. In China earthworm broth is considered both good food and good medicine. Turkish women wolf down worms in massive quantities to help them pack on the flesh that their men find so attractive. And, according to Calvin Schwabe, Gaddie's North American Bait Farms in California sponsors a contest that produces hundreds of wormy recipes every year. Gaddie likes them best in oatmeal cookies. They're good dried as well, it seems. Taste just like shredded wheat.

In Mexico honey ants, resembling big yellow currants, are a must at country weddings. In Zanzibar termites are ground up with sugar and banana flour into a sweet nougat-like paste. In Thailand there's a beetle that decimates the country's coconut and sugar palms. But the Thais don't panic. Nor do they spray. They swarm into the countryside to catch the little critters. Then they eat them.

There's so much food available to us that, for whatever reasons, imagined or invented, we refuse to eat. Calvin Schwabe reflects sadly on this wastefulness. He deplores our pig-headed refusal to open our minds, and our mouths, to the myriad, albeit unfamiliar, possibilities around us.

Jeffrey Steingarten takes up the same theme in his book *The Man Who Ate Everything*. He, after all, learned to love those "oil-soaked, leathery" strips of "rank and briny flesh" called anchovies. Anchovies were right up there with lard, kimchi and desserts served up in Indian restaurants on Steingarten's list of *foods I wouldn't touch even if I were starving on a desert island until absolutely everything else runs out.* Then, with this off his chest, he goes on to insist that we can all learn to love the food we think we hate. Including anchovies.

I'm not so sure. It seems to me that we've pretty much made up our minds on the subject of anchovies. You either love them—as I do—or you don't. They are pungent and powerful and decidedly on the fishy side, qualities unlikely to convince the skeptic for whom the highest compliment that one could pay to any fish is that it doesn't taste like fish at all.

Nonetheless, Steingarten proves his point. His personal anchovy epiphany came in the form of bagna cauda, a term derived from the Italian *bagno caldo,* which means "hot bath." And that's exactly what it is—a hot dip made with olive oil, butter, garlic and anchovies and served with raw vegetables. I'm not sure about bagna cauda. Nor is Elizabeth David, who, rather ominously, advises the less-resilient among us to approach this dish with extreme caution. Maybe my own anchovy-initiation offering would serve you better.

Easy-to-Love Anchovy Sauce for Pasta

Not a single anchovy had passed my lips before I met Chris. I wasn't afraid of them really—they'd just never come my way. And this is the dish, a mutual favourite, that gave me a taste of what I'd been missing.

8 to 10 anchovy fillets (in oil)
½ cup extra-virgin olive oil
Freshly ground black pepper

Drain the anchovies and chop them up. In a heavy saucepan, heat the oil at a medium-high setting. When it is very hot add the anchovies and mash them into the oil, along with the pepper, until you have a paste. Serve hot over cooked spaghetti or linguine. Makes ½ cup sauce, enough for ½ pound of pasta.

Do You Know What You're Eating?

What *are* sweetbreads?

I ask because when the question was put to me I answered confidently: brains. Calf's brains, lamb's brains, whatever—they're brains. I was wrong. So I did a little survey to see if anyone else had a better handle on this mystery meat than I.

I got a mixed response: pancreas (lots of votes for pancreas); testicles; panettone; esophagus; Bath buns; glands (the whole gamut of glands, thyroid and mammary being the top contenders); spleen; organs in general, vital and otherwise . . . and on it went.

Even the experts can't agree. According to *Larousse Gastronomique,* sweetbreads are thymus glands. Alan Davidson in *The Oxford Companion to Food* states confidently that "sweetbreads is a butcher's term which covers both the thymus gland and the pancreas of a young animal." And the pancreas, he adds, is "preferred by many." Calvin Schwabe says that sweetbreads taste very much like testicles, and infinitely better than pancreas, but they are neither: they are thymus glands. Waverley Root admits to the existence of "pancreatic sweetbreads" but he personally has never encountered such a thing.

I asked Chris. He didn't hesitate: thymus. I asked the waiter at the fancy restaurant where I had just ordered them. What I'd ordered, he assured me, was definitely a thymus gland. In this case, the thymus of a young lamb, *ris d'agneau*. The other highly prized *ris* is *de veau*, the thymus from a calf. Our waiter, executing a little blow-kiss with his fingertips, assured me I would enjoy this exquisite delicacy very much. I needed little convincing. It came in a Calvados sauce, after all.

And good it was. It's a tender little morsel, the thymus. "Sweet" as in rich. And "bread" as in morsel—a reference from centuries ago. The word *unctuous* comes to mind because unctuous they surely were. As does the term *euphemism*: *sweetbreads* has a decidedly tastier ring than *thymus*, don't you think?

My next question, after our waiter was out of earshot, was "What's a thymus? Do you know where *your* thymus is?"

My sweetbread-wise dinner partner indicated a vaguely midsection area, sort of below his heart and above his tummy. He was partly right. At least, that's where his thymus *used* to be. The fact is, if you're a post-pubescent creature of any description, you will search in vain for that delicious little thymus gland of yours. It begins to shrivel up during adolescence until it's a mere shadow of its former self in later years.

The same is true for all animals. In lamb and veal, however, the gland is a dual-compartment affair: an elongated section low in the throat that is connected by a tube to the larger, even better-tasting nut-shaped part (*noix*) near the heart. It plays a role in the formation of the immune system and, according to Waverley Root, is also thought to have something to do with an animal's sexual development. In other words, where the thymus is concerned, size matters.

I was getting into deep water here. I didn't really want to know about the sex life of barnyard creatures. But curiosity prodded me on. Why are sweetbreads so hard to come by? They're a rare treat in even the finest of restaurants. And they're simply not to be found in the offal department where I shop. The answer seems to be twofold. Sweetbreads are notoriously time consuming and complicated to prepare—a labour of love for the chef in a busy kitchen. And they're extremely perishable, so shelf life is measured in hours and long-distance travel is out of the question.

So what are we to make of all this? All I can tell you with absolute certainty is: sweetbreads, like hens' teeth, are a rarity; they are devilishly expensive, in restaurants, at least; they taste wonderful, like tender little dumplings; they go specially well with a delicate, boozy sauce; they're an endless source of lively debate. And, until the experts are of one mind, mine is made up: sweetbreads are thymus glands. Pancreas is pancreas. And, until a suitable euphemism can be found, testicles are off the menu.

Another puzzler: who invented haggis? And why did they bother?

Answer: good questions.

The origins of haggis are sketchy. What we do know is that the Scots have set aside a special day for this particular feast: January 29, Robbie Burns Day. Robbie-the-poet was very partial to haggis, it seems, a predilection baffling in the extreme when you read the recipe.

Take the stomach bag of a sheep, turn it inside out and scrape it clean with a knife. Leave it to soak in salted water overnight. Then boil it for 1½ hours leaving the windpipe to hang over the edge of the pot so all the impurities may escape.

Who knows how a windpipe came to be attached to a stomach? It sounds like a recipe for chronic indigestion to me. But that's what my source, *Out of Old Nova Scotia Kitchens*, tells us. However, having got the thing in the pot I think we should see the project through. Besides, it's pretty straightforward from here on in. It's the old boil-in-a-bag technology. Except you do the bagging.

First you have to remove the windpipe, then you can start filling your stomach: heart, lungs, liver—chopped up, of course, or you'll end up with a most unattractive presentation. You'll need some suet as well, along with oatmeal, grated onion and some salt and pepper. When the stomach bag is full, sew it up and boil the whole thing for three hours.

Now, according to my haggis authority, you're going to need a mess of clapshot to go along with it. Clapshot, or tatties 'n neeps, is simply potatoes and turnips boiled up and mashed together with salt and pepper and a bit of butter. You're also going to need bagpipes. And Scotch whisky.

I happen to love the skirl of the pipes, a sound so haunting and lusty it squeezes my heart into a small ball and brings tears to my eyes. I love Scotch whisky too. It gives me the courage I need to eat haggis.

When you've lined up a piper to provide the appropriate fanfare for your entrance with the haggis, you'll have to brief your guests on the protocol for this pivotal moment in the proceedings. They must stand on their chairs with one foot on the table, and as the pipes play and you hold aloft your magnificent sausage they are to toss back a glass of whisky then smash their glasses onto the floor.

What fun! And it's while you're scooping up shards of broken glass you'll ask the inevitable question: whose idea was this anyway?

I have a theory about how it all started. I think it was a case of barbecue burn-out. After several thousand years of charred meat from the fire pit, the more discriminating among the cave population yearned for something a little more refined.

"Gosh, dear," the hungry hunter might have said, "I've got all this offal stuff, bits and pieces from the sheep I brought home last night. Sure would be good to have a nice boil-up for a change."

"No problem," said the plucky cave woman. "This left-over stomach might work. I was going to use it as a purse— but maybe we could boil up the offal stuff in that!"

And out she went in search of the clay to make a pot, and the rest is history.

But there's another question. What inspired the creation of the bagpipes? And how did the pipes and the haggis become so inextricably linked?

Well . . . just a thought, but here's how I see it. Our enter-prising cave couple, having created this new taste sensation, might have wanted to herald the occasion with a little festive music. And a quick search through the rubble of leftover sheep bits would have turned up the perfect solution. A piper's bag *au naturel*: the bladder.

Bingo! We've got a bag. We've got one slightly used, par-boiled windpipe. And I suspect that with a bit of surgical thread and a few lengths of bamboo there would be music in the air before long. And that, I submit, is how it came to be that a sheep's stomach was, once upon a time, escorted to the table by its bladder.

A Proper Breakfast

There's a time and a place for extreme cuisine. The occasional tongue sandwich at lunch goes down fine. Haggis for dinner is prudently confined to one meal a year. But there's an unwritten rule about breakfast. You don't mess with it. I have my way. You have yours. I think we should respect that.

Take toast as an example. There are two schools of thought on this: the British way, and my way.

In England toast is delivered, upright and stiff with the cold, in little silver racks. This is not correct. Toast should be crisp, yes, but not so crisp that you end up in a blizzard of crumbs and you can't hear yourself think for the racket between your ears. It should also be hot in order for that big splodge of butter to slide, unimpeded, from crust to crust. Then you apply the

Marmite. Or, depending on your mood, peanut butter. You do not trowel cold butter on cold toast and then wad on the marmalade. Some people do this. But it is not correct.

Eggs, should you choose to have eggs, are to be gently simmered, Grandad's way: for three minutes or until the toast pops up. There are as many ways to cook an egg as there are ways to skin a cat. But only one is correct.

Then there is the all-important business of coffee. The day's first cup should be relished in solitude. If the dog attempts to engage you in conversation, send him packing. If a human tries this, refer him to the dog. Your coffee should be of the high-test caffeinated variety, otherwise things will fall apart. Some people like to wake up under their own steam. This is impossible.

Of all meals breakfast is the one self-indulgent occasion of the day when personal ritual is sacrosanct. Which is why, when the muesli issue hijacked my morning, I was less than receptive.

It had arrived on the premises unbidden. The perpetrator, a Swiss friend with a big heart, had brought it as a gift when she came for a visit.

"This is *real* muesli," she announced. "What's called muesli here in Canada bears no resemblance to the real thing."

Besides, I was informed, *muesli* isn't pronounced "moos-ly," which means "small mouse" in Swiss. Nor is it correct to say "mews-ly." *Muesli* rhymes with *fiercely*. Got that? And *muffin* rhymes with *ratatouille*. Clever stuff.

The lesson continued over coffee. The original concoction, I found out, was named *Birchermuesli* after Dr. Max Bircher-Benner, who ran a spa in Zurich and believed fiercely (rhymes with *muesli*) in the virtues of a vegetarian diet. Bircher (pronounced "Beer-ker") used a combination of uncooked grains, nuts and various fruits as well as milk or yogurt.

Ever the obliging host, I suggested we whip up a batch then and there. But no. Authentic *Birchermuesli* is not simply served up with milk or yogurt. It is soaked in it, preferably overnight, so it has a chance to morph into a suitably stodgy mush. Which is only to be expected when you consider that *muesli* is derived from a Swiss-German word, *mus,* which means "pulpy" or "puréed." Or, come to think of it, "mess."

We followed approved muesli protocol. We assembled oats and nuts and fruit and yogurt and let it sit overnight. To be on the safe side, I got up in the wee small hours to fortify myself with a Marmite-and-cholesterol sandwich just in case things didn't work out.

They didn't. In fact, our *mus* looked decidedly *mus*sier than it had the night before. Like wallpaper paste with lumps. My friend pronounced it perfect. The dog loved it. I thanked my friend for presenting me with this early-morning diversion and reached for the cornflakes. I'd learned something: *muesli*, roughly translated, means "cereal killer" and has no place at my breakfast table.

Crunchy Granola

Pronounced exactly as spelled. And needs no soaking. After eggs, this is my favourite way to start the day—more wholesome and tastier by far than those production-line breakfast fillers you buy. It pays to make a big batch so it's there to snack on, like trail mix, when you get the munchies.

3 cups old-fashioned rolled oats

1 cup wheat germ

1 cup unsalted sunflower seeds, hulled

¾ cup chopped almonds

¾ cup chopped hazelnuts

½ cup sesame seeds

½ cup skim milk powder

½ cup vegetable oil

¼ cup honey

1½ cups raisins

½ cup chopped dried apricots

½ cup dried cranberries, cherries or other dried fruit

Preheat oven to 300°F.

Spread the oats evenly in a large shallow pan and bake for 15 minutes.

In a large bowl combine the wheat germ, sunflower seeds, almonds, hazelnuts, sesame seeds and milk powder. Warm the oil and the honey together in a small pan and add to the mixture in the bowl. Stir well. Add the toasted oats and combine thoroughly. Spread the mixture in two large shallow pans and toast in the oven, stirring once halfway through, for 15 to 20 minutes or until it's golden brown. Let it cool.

Add the raisins, apricots and any other dried fruit you are using. Tightly covered in Mason jars, the granola keeps well in the fridge for months.

Makes about 2½ quarts.

I mention Marmite as if it were just another option in my morning routine. This is misleading. I am addicted to Marmite. And breakfast is just one of many essential Marmite moments in my day.

Oddly enough, most North Americans haven't the faintest idea what Marmite is. Or if they do they can't for the life of them imagine why anyone would want to eat it. Marmite is the offal of the vegetable world.

Like cold toast and Eccles cakes, Marmite is a British thing. Writing in the *Guardian* on the occasion of Marmite's one-hundedth birthday in 2001, Laura Barton acknowledges the hold this "Holy Grail of foodstuffs" has on her countrymen. She tells the story of Paul Ridout, a British backpacker kidnapped by Kashmiri separatists in 1994. Upon his release, and safely back home in England, Ridout's first order of business was to dig into a stack of Marmite-enhanced toast.

"It was pretty good," he says. "It's just one of those things—you get out of the country and it's all you think about."

The sticky black reaches of a Marmite jar might seem an unlikely source of solace, but Paul Ridout's instincts were good ones. Marmite is a powerhouse of vitamins, especially the B lineup. It is made from the yeast left over from the brewing process, which explains why Marmite's birthplace was just downriver from the Bass Brewery on Burton-on-Trent. It's still there. And much of the yeast still comes from

Bass. So even if you're not a Marmite enthusiast you've got to admit its credentials are impeccable.

But what *is* it about Marmite anyway? This gooey sludge that looks like shoe polish and tastes, as one skeptic puts it, "like licking paint." I can't really give you a satisfactory answer except to say that Marmite delivers a taste hit like nothing else. And it is definitely habit forming: the more you eat, the more you need to eat.

Laura Barton says: "Spreading Marmite is an art form. It has to be done thinly. In fact, not just thinly, but t-h-i-n-l-y. This isn't strawberry jam or peanut butter. This is a spread that can make grown men weep."

Laura Barton is right—to a point. The Marmite buff in-training is generally content with the less-is-more rule—the lightest lick, the thinnest skim on a water biscuit or a slice of buttered bread. And Marmite minimalism can see you through for years. But over time, as scar tissue forms and taste buds falter, that yeasty rush becomes harder and harder to sustain. The Marmite gets laid on thicker and thicker until toast with Marmite becomes Marmite with only the skimpiest of underpinnings to legitimize one's raging cravings. Soon you drop the props and eat it straight until it's gone. That's when grown men weep. And grown women can be found scouring sustenance from the curves of an empty Marmite jar with a teaspoon. It's pathetic actually.

All of this must seem quite daft to those of you who have never experienced Marmite's peculiar charms. I can only urge you—"you" being about 90 percent of the world's population at last count—to pluck up your courage and give it a try. Then try, try again. It's so good for you! Marmite is fat free, sugar free and 100 percent vegetarian. This comes as a surprise to many who see the little stew pot, *marmite* in French, on the label and think "beef." Bovril is a beef-based product. Marmite isn't.

There's another thing that every Marmite addict knows: there are no substitutes. Vegemite, an Australian product, is a flabby imitation of the real thing, a different taste altogether. Compared to the intense, sharp-sour yeastiness of Marmite, Vegemite approaches the palate almost apologetically, as if it would like to be Marmite but lacks the courage.

I have a jar of Marmite in my cupboard that speaks volumes about my fondness for the stuff. This is not your standard-issue, egg-size jar of Marmite. This is the heavyweight (500-gram) version. Think of a large turnip. Think of enough Marmite to feed a small village for a year. And ask yourself not if I have a problem but how expeditiously and with what measure of relish and dedication I can lick it.

None for Me, Thanks

There are two foods that, as an opinionated ten-year-old, I declared unfit for this human's consumption: cauliflower with cheese sauce, and tapioca.

The cauliflower aversion was more of a hunch than anything. I had simply caught a whiff of it cooking and, prone to dramatics as I was at that self-absorbed age, I instantly expressed my revulsion all over my mother's prized Oriental carpet. I've not touched the stuff since. Naked cauliflower—steamed, raw, whatever—is fine. I'm very fond of it, in fact. Which is utterly irrational because I'm sure it was the smell of over-boiled cauliflower, not the cheese sauce, that set me off in the first place.

Tapioca is a different story. I have never plucked up the courage to revisit those slithery, slip-slidey lumps of stuff that remind me still of something extruded from the nether end of a frog.

Having said that, I have to confess that I really hadn't the faintest idea what I was talking about. What *is* tapioca, anyway? A starch of some sort, I supposed. But tasting of nothing at all except the insufferable sweetness that defined the pudding-to-gag-on from my childhood.

So, curious, I did the unthinkable. I bought some. Then I rooted through my books to find out what it was. *The Oxford Companion to Food* confirmed the obvious: "Tapioca pudding is sometimes despised by the ignorant, that is to say persons who have no knowledge of how good [it is] when properly made. Also, when tapioca is cooked in milk it becomes translucent and jelly-like, causing children to detect a resemblance between it and frog spawn."

Frog spawn! See? I told you so.

Tapioca, I learned, comes from cassava, which is also called manioc and yuca. Or, come to think of it, maniac and yucky, depending on your position vis-à-vis the cooked product. Cassava is a shrub cultivated throughout the tropical regions of the world. Its leaves are edible but it's the large starchy, cigar-shaped roots that are the dietary staple for millions.

There are two varieties of cassava: bitter and sweet. The

bitter kind is bitter because—guess what?—it's laced with cyanide. And this variety, you'll be thrilled to know, is the one we eat. But not to worry. Tapioca may be disgusting but it's not going to kill you. American Indians discovered long ago that the root's poison is quickly dissipated when it is soaked and cooked.

Generally, the cassava root is used to make a flour—*farinha* in Brazil, *gari* in Algeria. In Africa it's cooked and pummelled into a kind of porridge called *foo-foo,* which sounds adorable but—again, a hunch—I suspect isn't. In the Caribbean the juice from the root is combined with sugar and spices to make a pungent, syrupy sauce known as *cassareep.* But what we lucky folk are most likely to encounter are the little pellets of starch (*tipioceto*) that are extracted from the liquid (*tipioca*) during pressing. It's called "pearl" tapioca. Which is what I bought.

The label actually said: *Tapioca (Sago).* That was curious because sago, though very like tapioca, is definitely *not* tapioca. It comes from the pithy trunk of the sago palm, a tree that grows wild in the swampy areas of Southeast Asia. When I pointed out this discrepancy to the shopkeeper I was quietly but firmly corrected. In the Philippines, I was told, sago and tapioca are one and the same.

I abandoned the debate and went home to make pudding. Several puddings, as it turned out. The first one failed. It looked like glue laced with buckshot. Apparently I was using regular tapioca, not the quick-cooking kind, a nuance the recipe had failed to clarify. My second attempt was a spectacular flop as well because I didn't know you had to soak the stuff. On the third go I got a pudding.

I tasted it and passed the bowl to my husband. He tasted it and passed the bowl to the dog.

Case closed. The proof, if we needed any, is in the pudding.

Home-wrecker Soup

I've never eaten bird's nest soup and doubt I ever will. I live on the wrong side of the world, for one thing. I'd have to go to China or Taiwan and pay $75 a bowl for the privilege and that seems highly unlikely. Besides, I've always felt a tad uneasy about the prospect of a bolus of twigs and moss making its way, like a hedgehog through a turnstile, down my throat. So why is it so sought after? And how did some bird's nest end up in the soup pot in the first place? It was all very curious. I did some digging to find out more.

As it turns out, I was wrong about the ingredient list. Bird's nest soup is made with a lightly spiced chicken broth or consommé base, and bird spit. That's good to know. I was also reassured to discover that the nests that deliver the bird spit are not the common garden-variety structures assembled by your average backyard robin. The home-owner is a small swallow-like bird, native to the Philippines and New Guinea, called the white-nest swiftlet.

His story is not a happy one. The male selects a home site in the dark reaches of mountain and seaside caves where he crafts a shallow, teacup-shaped nest with a pasty secretion from his salivary glands. As these spaghetti-like strands dry they adhere to each other and to the cave walls like an oyster to a rock. If he is lucky, he will mate and produce one clutch of little swiftlets before their home is snatched from under them. In many cases, nests are taken before eggs are even laid. Sometimes baby birds are thrown away.

It is folly, I'm told, to sentimentalize. Who am I to imagine what a homeless swiftlet feels? But I do. And I imagine the worst—fear, rage, puzzlement, despair. What I can't imagine is that a creature thus violated would feel nothing at all.

One must, however grudgingly, tip one's hat to the nimble-footed nest snatchers. This thievery is not easily accomplished. The caves are deep and dark. Some, as vast as cathedrals, can house colonies as large as a million birds. Workers, often in bare feet, climb rickety bamboo ladders to reach nests ninety feet above the cave floor.

Not surprisingly, the swiftlet population has been declining dramatically. Efforts to protect it have failed because of the profits to be made: nests can sell for $2,000 a kilo. So the caves are often protected from poachers by armed guards, and the risk of a shipment being hijacked in transit is very real. As a result, the bird's nest trade is shrouded in secrecy and controlled by a few well-connected and hugely wealthy businessmen who, although their enterprise is entirely legal, prefer to publicize their involvement as little as possible.

Why is this tiny, snow-white nest so sought after? There are two reasons. The first, reputedly, is the culinary experience itself. This is hardly surprising: the presence of bird spit in my soup bowl would get my attention right off the bat. And the presentation, an occasion of high ceremony in some quarters, is noteworthy as well: one prized accompaniment to this venerable dish is snake venom, which, to the chagrin of the uninitiated, is delivered to the table by the snake himself. Happily, this living condiment dispenser is escorted to the event by his personal trainer, a man with a sure grip and a practiced touch. With a deft squeeze he engages the snake, who spritzes the soup with the mandatory dribble of poison. Then, I suppose, you eat it.

The other reason for man's devotion to the swiflet's nest is the mythology that has grown up around it. For centuries the Chinese believed that this tiny bird ate nothing but the windblown foam from the sea. Therefore, they reasoned, eating its nest was like absorbing the iodine from the seaweed, the ocean's shimmering phosphorescence, and the concentrated essence of everything this tiny bird stands for: devotion, endurance, power and virility.

I like that. I like the idea of connecting so strongly with another living creature. I like the notion of this extraordinary little bird being the embodiment of the power and magic and constancy of the sea. I just wish we could embrace these lofty thoughts without eating him out of house and home in the process.

Your Bus Driver Recommends...

Bird's nest soup aside, I wholeheartedly agree with Jeffrey Steingarten and Calvin Schwabe on the importance of keeping an open mind where food is concerned. In fact, I've made it a policy to eat with relish and gratitude just about anything that comes my way. And, for the most part, my surprises have been happy ones. But my open-mind, open-mouth approach to the unexpected hasn't always served me well. Fran Lebowitz sounded the warning.

"People have been cooking and eating for thousands of years, so if you are the very first to have thought of adding fresh lime juice to scalloped potatoes try to understand that there must be a reason for this."

What follows is a mealtime serving suggestion, word for word, that came my way quite by accident from perfect strangers on a bus in downtown Vancouver.

The driver falls into conversation with one of his passengers, a small woman with a big voice who is seated nearby. They're discussing food. I am instantly alert. She's tired. She's hungry. It's been a long day.

"I'm gonna soak in a tub, play a few games of Super Mario and send out for a pizza." She sighs. "I could cook myself a steak," she says, "but I'm on a diet."

The driver thinks about this.

"I'm off meat," the woman says. "Meat fills you out and I don't need filling out."

"You like shrimp?" asks the driver.

"Sure."

"I got a dish—if you like shrimp, you'll love this. I make it all the time."

"Oh yeah? I got shrimp. Have I got shrimp!" Her arms describe the measure of her booty—about the size of a king-size pillow. "Bulk shrimp. Love it."

"Okay. So's here's what you do," says the driver. We're stopped at a light now so the intricacies of shrimp cookery are given his undivided attention.

"You can make a white sauce, right?" he asks.

"Sure."

"Melt some butter, whisk in a little flour . . ."

"Yeah yeah. I can do white sauce."

"Okay. So you add some milk, right? And let it bubble away for a bit . . ."

"Yeah yeah."

"So you got your white sauce . . ." Traffic is moving now and he's distracted for a minute. I'll have to change seats if I'm going to stay on top of this. I sidle closer and pretend to be watching for my stop.

"So you throw the shrimp into your white sauce and mix it up, okay? Now what you do—you ready for this? This is great . . ."

The little woman is on the edge of her seat. Me too.

"You need a papaya."

A *papaya?* I bite my tongue.

"A *papaya?*" says the woman.

"And you slice it in half, okay? Now you take a spoon and scoop out the seeds . . ."

"The seeds are black, right?"

"Right. But what I do is I scoop a little deeper. You know what I'm saying? Make more room in the papaya."

"Okay.'

"So you take your shrimp in your white sauce and you pile it up in the papaya, okay?"

"You kidding?" the woman says. He's kidding, I'm thinking.

"And you bake it—I dunno, twenty minutes, maybe? Maybe more. In the oven."

"Yeah?"

"It's great. It . . . is . . . so . . . *good!*"

"Baked papaya, huh?"

"Really. It's, like, this warm, sweet papaya, right? With the shrimp? And the sauce? Fantastic."

"So cool. That sounds so cool."

"It is. It is very cool."

"I'm making it. Tonight. I am." She's bouncing in her seat.

"You'll have to get a papaya though," says the driver.

"No problem. I'll get a papaya." She's looking quite dreamy now. "And for dessert—let me tell you about dessert."

We—the driver and I—are all ears.

"Fried bananas. Mango ice cream. And butterscotch sauce."

"Yeah?"

"It is soooo *good.*"

"No kidding."

"Or you can do chocolate sauce. Chocolate's good."

It wasn't my stop but I got off anyway. I had some shopping to do: mango ice cream, bananas, butterscotch sauce. I wasn't ready for the shrimp-stuffed papaya experiment yet. It's like lime juice in scalloped potatoes. I had my doubts.

6

People and Other Mealtime Curiosities

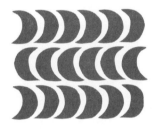

*In general, [my children] refused
to eat anything that hadn't danced on TV.*

ERMA BOMBECK

Oh No! There's Butter on the Honey Knife!

I want to ride a scooter and swim the length of the lake through duckweed when there's a child at my side. I become an instant expert on baseball stats, banana slugs and who killed whom with a lead pipe in the library. And I am touched in tender spots I'd forgotten I possessed when I'm presented with the Harry Potter book they know I've not yet read. But, all things being equal, I'd rather eat with the grown-ups.

Kids are the ultimate appetite suppressants, and I was recently prescribed two, every day, for a week. One was called Danny, the other Drew.

Danny, seven, is our grandson. He has the dreamy, pink-cheeked face of an angel. He can read an entire *Goosebumps* book in an hour, shuffle a pack of cards so that an ace always lands in his lap and wash behind his ears without getting his face wet. He also has some firmly entrenched notions about food.

We don't see him often. He lives two thousand miles away. So if you've not had to squeeze mustard onto a slice of bologna for a while you tend to get it on the lettuce by mistake. And you forget that orange juice with pulp in it will cause a small child to faint dead away on the spot. A meal

163

with Danny and his friend Drew was like negotiating your way through customs with various undeclared banned substances. You learn to be cagey.

"Does this fish have bones in it?"

"Bones? Have you ever heard of a B.C. fish with bones?"

"What's feta?"

"It's like Velveeta. Only white."

We made pasta—regular pasta. They hate "the stuff that looks like radiators." In a cloud of flour and a tangle of elbows we joined forces at the pasta machine to roll it out. The kids loved the novelty of this and concentrated mightily on the task at hand. It was the meal itself that put a damper on things. What materialized on their plates was, apparently, too gross for words.

I'd made tomato sauce for the pasta, a decision taken after in-depth research as to what constituted acceptable food and what didn't. They liked tomatoes. But not in salads. And definitely *not* in pizza. And, yes, they liked tomato sauce all right but—and this was offered up with deceptive offhandedness—they actually liked "white sauce" better. I gambled on tomato. And lost.

The handcrafted pasta was a hit. However, the logistics of eating it were excruciating in the extreme, as each slippery strand had to be painstakingly extricated from, and purged of, a sauce that, it seems, had been sullied with all manner of contaminants.

"Aaarrgh!" said Danny. "It's got *seeds* in it!"

"What's this green stuff?" asked Drew.

"Basil."

"Yuck!"

The pasta deconstruction was accompanied by humming and a display of on-the-spot calisthenics that included rhythmic leg swings, lumbar stretches, buttock rolls and foot jiggling. We were glad of the humming, encouraged it in fact, as these musical interludes were punctuated by the slick, wet suck and slap of noodles being vacuumed up from plate to maw. I passed the salad.

Once again, our resident food inspectors discovered a whole new cache of of suspect ingredients. Danny considered lettuce to be marginally edible. But not with dressing on it. Or if it had cohabited, even briefly, with an avocado, which this particular lettuce indubitably had. Drew had already made clear his position on vegetables. They're okay all mixed together, like in a salad. But not separate. Not like, you know, on their own. *This* salad, however, he wasn't sure about. He extracted a crouton from amongst the poisons surrounding it.

These were homemade, industrial-strength croutons, spectacularly crunchy and an unqualified hit. So now the slip-slap-suck of the noodle ensemble was accompanied by a vigorous performance from the percussion section. Conversation was out of the question. They made a meal of croutons and sauce-free pasta and seemed quite content. The next night we went out for pizza.

We're offered two choices—vegetarian or Mediterranean. The vegetarian option is rejected out of hand. And what, they ask plaintively, is *Mediterranean?* I can't prevaricate. Feta—*Oh, no!* Green peppers—*No way!* Olives. They're struck dumb. But you can pick them off, I say, and they settle in for a foraging session. They peel and pluck and eventually reassemble an acceptable pizza facsimile consisting of crust and congealed mozzarella.

We picked our way through a variety of culinary land mines over the next few days. Such horrors as runny eggs, raspberries—*more seeds!*—freckled bananas, cantaloupe, and butter on the honey knife.

We made popcorn, watched *Shrek* one more time, did a hummingbird inventory and then we went camping . . .

I'm not into puzzles as a rule. But puzzles come with the territory when you go camping with kids.

Here's one. It's a misty West Coast morning in late July and four travellers have assembled in a forest clearing in anticipation of the day's first meal. The group consists of two small boys with very large appetites and two sleep-deprived adults with lame backs, a severely diminished caffeine count and little stomach for the task at hand. The adults present the menu options: bacon, eggs, two rather puny sausages, home fries, toast and coffee. (That's coffee for two—high-octane, black and the sooner the better.)

I should note that toast is a newly discovered camping luxury for us. All you need is one camp stove burner and a fold-up wire rack that can turn four slices of bread into four slices of randomly charred toast in just under five minutes.

The youngsters approve the menu—with a few refinements they are quick to point out. They like their bacon crisp and in large quantities. The adults make it known that they prefer their bacon slightly *under*-crisp. But they also like it in large quantities. Three diners agree on two eggs each. Fried. The one holdout, Drew, is dead set against fried eggs, citing the sick-making slipperiness of the yolk

166

when prepared in this manner. Scrambled eggs (two, please) are now added to the cooks' list of things to do all at once. Two sausages get eight thumbs up, a puzzle in itself. And as for the home fries—well, they meet with guarded approval: *if* they don't actually touch the eggs. And *if* they are accompanied by ample splats of ketchup. The egg-clearance restrictions are agreed to, but the total absence of ketchup in this particular neck of the woods necessitates a rethink on the home fries front. The result: three orders of home fries, not four. And everyone's up for toast.

Let's recap. Four double orders of bacon done this way and that; eight eggs (six fried, two scrambled); two inadequate sausages (divided four ways); home fries times three; and four orders of toast.

Here is the puzzle: how do two frazzled cooks, working in tandem with a two-burner camp stove, two small frying pans, one saucepan and a toasting rack complete the assignment to the specifications outlined above so that all four diners can sit down to a flawlessly prepared and seamlessly presented morning meal with no blips, slips or tears?

Can it be done? Should it even be attempted? Where's Cap'n Crunch when we need him?

Stumped? Here's the solution:

Melt a hefty knob of butter in the saucepan over Burner One. Add sliced, cooked potatoes and let them sizzle away, stirring when you get a chance, until golden brown. Meantime, in Frying Pan A, on Burner Two, sizzle bacon (Batch 1) until crisp. Set aside. On Burner Two you may now fry the two sausages (divided into four servings) along with the bacon (Batch 2) in Frying Pan B, until the bacon is semi-crisp. Reduce the heat on Burner One and carefully lay the contents of Frying Pan B on top of the contents in the saucepan. Now lay the contents of Frying Pan A in a distinct layer on top of the contents of Frying Pan B, which are keeping warm on top of the contents of the saucepan. Break six eggs into Frying Pan A and fry over low heat on Burner Two. Whisk two eggs and pour into Frying Pan B, which you now place on top of Frying Pan A (on Burner Two) and stir gently until nicely scrambled. Frying Pans A and B now go on top of saucepan on Burner One, allowing you to engage the toaster rack on Burner Two. When toast is done, dismantle stacked pots and pans on Burner One and serve.

When the kids go back home to Ontario my appetite kicks in and life goes on. But I'm oddly out of sorts. I want to hunt for hermit crabs, make popcorn and play Clue "just once more before bedtime." There's no one to do a hummingbird count with. No one to follow a slug's progress from petunia patch to basil pot. It's all very grown up, marvellously civilized, and no damn fun at all.

Fresh, No-Cook Tomato Sauce

This is a wonderful pasta sauce to take camping as it will keep nicely in a cooler for 2 or 3 days. It's served at room (ambient campsite) temperature over steaming-hot pasta so you have a meal in minutes with minimal fuss. I make this well ahead of time so the flavours have a chance to get acquainted. And of course it's best when summer tomatoes are fully ripe and fresh off the vine.

(Warning: this sauce contains ingredients that small children may find offensive: raw tomatoes, tomato seeds, green stuff and various suspect herbs and spices.)

4 to 6 large ripe tomatoes, chopped
⅓ large, sweet onion (I like Vidalia), chopped
1 clove garlic, minced
12 (more if you like) large fresh basil leaves, torn into pieces
1 tablespoon chopped fresh oregano (or 1 teaspoon dried)
2 teaspoons chopped fresh rosemary (or ½ teaspoon dried)
½ teaspoon salt
Fresh-cracked black pepper
½ cup good-quality olive oil
2 tablespoons fresh-squeezed lemon juice
1 pound pasta

Put all ingredients (except pasta) in a bowl, combine well, and let sit for an hour or so, longer if that suits. (If you want to fuss around peeling and seeding the tomatoes, that's your call. I prefer the keep-it-simple approach myself.)

Cook pasta in lightly salted water until al dente, drain, toss with the sauce and serve.

Serves 4.

Mind Your P's and Q's

I think it's time to brush up on our table manners. A quaint notion, some would say. Redundant even, in this eat-and-run age when fewer and fewer people ever make it to the table at all. But before we do away with table manners entirely, a quick review of the basics, just for old times' sake, seems in order.

Bennett Cerf defined good manners as "the noise you don't make when you're eating soup." And a children's book on etiquette from 1701 offered this advice: "Smell not to thy Meat, nor move it to thy Nose; turn it not the other side upward to view it upon the Plate."

Very sensible all around. Much depends, of course, on the company you keep. You'd be permitted a certain amount of leeway if you were dining with Bedouins, for instance. In her book *The Rituals of Dinner*, Margaret Visser describes one convention of desert hospitality: Bedouin custom demands that the hungry must be fed even if they're your enemy. However, ill will can sometimes override good manners, and disgruntled guests have been known to take up handfuls of food, smear it contemptuously over their closed mouths and pitch it into the dust at their feet. One witness to this, a traveller in Iraq during the 1930s, reported that the guests, hungry though they obviously were, expressed their displeasure, then strode off wiping their hands on their clothes and in their hair.

You could try this next time the hospitality isn't to your liking. But personally, I prefer the approach of the noblewoman La Baronne Staffe, who set the tone in nineteenth-century France. "If dishes are failures, you do not notice," says the baronne. "You eat bravely what is offered, as if it were good."

The French are very sticky about this. You do not criticize the food offered. Nor, they insist, do you praise it. There are fragile nuances at work here. Margaret Visser explains: a reverent silence is in order when a splendid dish is presented—a few muted murmurs of approval at the most. But to gasp in wonder or squeal with joy would definitely be out of line. It suggests you want lots. It could also, we are warned, imply surprise. *You* made *that?* Tactless in the extreme.

Another thing: the host must never praise his or her own food. "One rejoices silently in one's success," the baronne observes sternly. I'd scrap that rule. I break it all the time anyway. *Oh, this is sooo good!* I say, never mind that I'm the cook and that everyone else at the table is maintaining the baronne's rule of discreet silence. No, we all need a congratulatory pat on the back from time to time, and a do-it-yourself pat is better than no pat at all.

And there have always been strict rules about vomiting. This from Erasmus nearly five hundred years ago in his treatise on manners, *De civilitate morum puerilium* (*On the Civility of the Behaviour of Boys*):

"Withdraw when you are going to vomit; vomiting is not shameful, but to have vomited through gluttony is disgusting." No argument there.

In North America, it was Emily Post who laid down the law on manners, with the publication, in 1922, of (the ponderously titled) *Etiquette in Society, in Business, in Politics and at Home.* Emily was stern and unambiguous, and her word held sway for a good part of the twentieth century: *never* stack the plates when clearing the table; *never* use your fingers to eat French fries (except when they're served with sandwiches); *never* lay a coloured tablecloth beneath a lace one lest the tacky undercloth show through—the equivalent, I suppose, of flaunting one's knickers in public.

Then, sixty years later, Miss Manners, aka Judith Martin, arrived on the scene and things lightened up considerably. What, she asks, does the gracious host do when a lady trips, lurches across a table and lands face first in a bowl of guacamole? What indeed?

Laugh. To do otherwise, according to Miss Manners, implies that "the lady did it all the time and her friends have gotten used to it." Right! Now good manners begin to make good sense. Our course is clear. After all, as Erasmus wisely pointed out: "The essence of good manners consists in freely pardoning the shortcomings of others although nowhere falling short yourself."

Lead by example. Don't cause discomfort to those who fall by the wayside. This is a wise and magnanimous approach to manners. The only tricky bit that I can see is the "falling short yourself" business. I've been known to fall short on occasion. Which is why I compiled my Ten Commandments of dos and don'ts for the table. You may find them helpful.

Thou shalt not play with thy food.

Neither shalt thou offer up Brussels sprouts unto the dog.

Or build mansions amongst the peas with thy mashed potatoes.

Thou shalt not spear fish nor meat nor fowl with one hand and take it up with the other.

Nor shalt thou deliver it unto thy mouth whilst food resideth there still.

Reach not for that which lieth beyond thy grasp or upon the floor or on thy neighbour's plate.

Also, I say unto you, butter not thy bread all in one go.

Nor strike thy brother or thy sister with sharp instruments.

Or show forth thy food or any portion thereof whilst thou doth chew.

Thou shalt keep thine elbows close by thy sides forever.

These were the Rules of the Table as I was taught them. And I have abided by them, for the most part, throughout my adult life. Except for the bit about butter all over. And one little slip-up—the aforementioned shortfall—which I'll confess to you now because I know I shall be pardoned when you understand the circumstances.

I played with my food. Actually, that's not entirely accurate. I helped myself to someone else's food and played with that. Even worse.

It happened one summer at a dinner party. There were six of us, an awkward gathering with little in common apart from a general lethargy brought on by the August heat. Our hostess had announced at the outset that she loathed cooking, so while her husband tended to the barbecue we groped for things to talk about. The conversation had lurched from the subject of root canals to pool disinfectants when the platter of steaks and corn on the cob appeared. The steaks were done to a turn, the corn tender and milky-sweet, and we bent to our task in contented silence. Then, with sighs all round, we gathered up the tattered threads of conversation once again.

Someone had just bought a weed-whacker and was regaling us with the delights of whacking weeds when the idea came to me.

"Did you know," I announced, "that I can read corn cobs?"

Even the weed-whacker fell silent. I offered up my wine glass for a refill.

"Yes," I said, "you can tell a lot from a person's empty corn cob."

And I did. I picked up the frayed cob from my neighbour's plate. I knew him only slightly so I had little inside information to draw on. But I had his corn cob. That was enough.

"You," I pronounced, fixing him with my all-seeing eye, "are a detail man. You probably work with numbers, crunching them out, lining them up. You do not take kindly to an interruption of routine. You get cranky when things don't go according to plan."

I was on to something here. The pinched set of his mouth spoke volumes.

"And," I continued, enjoying myself thoroughly by now, "you're prone to frequent bouts of indigestion." This seemed a safe bet. A sour stomach will pinch up a mouth every time.

The company was agog. But it had been all too easy. His

corn cob had been stripped in neatly ordered rows. He had broached it at one end and proceeded, with the obsessive purpose and precision of a drill master, to the other. None of that follow-the-melting-butter-with-your-nose routine for him. He turned out to be an insurance adjuster. And the ulcer problem, he assured me, was under control.

So far so good. Another shorn cob, that of a female guest, told a different story. It had been attacked randomly and with great gusto.

"Oh, yes," I said. "I identify with this."

I told her what I saw: jollity and bedlam. Lists made and lost. Library books overdue. Peanut butter on doorknobs.

She grinned. "That's me!" she said.

"There's more," I said. "The corn cob speaks to me of all manner of unrealized dreams and secret passions." A simple deduction: she was married to the insurance adjuster. She was the one with butter on her chin. The table fell silent. Mr. and Mrs. Insurance Adjuster consulted their watches. Our hostess, looking rattled, leaped to her feet, whisked up the telltale cobs and headed for the kitchen.

"So. What about those Blue Jays then, eh?" someone said.

That was fun, I thought. Fun and silly and remarkably revealing. Because of course you *can* "read" corn cobs. You can read so much of a person by the way they reach for and embrace the food that's put before them. After that evening, I added the eleventh commandment to the Rules of the Table:

Approacheth your food with gratitude and joy for howsoever ye shall eat so shall thy life unfold.

Men in Aprons

The Latin American food writer Elizabeth Lambert tells us the word *barbecue* derives from the Spanish *barbacoa,* a Taino Indian word for the rough framework used for drying meat over the fire. I have another theory. I think that *barbacoa* is an Indian word that, roughly translated, means "gathering place for men in aprons."

There are no scholarly data to back me up on this. Just an informal study of guys in general. What I've observed is that guys in general don't julienne carrots, coddle eggs, or make brownies. But where they really shine every time is at the barbecue. Men who have never rolled pastry or stirred a risotto stride confidently to centre stage when there's meat to be charred.

Why is this? Why, when women are designing bridges and performing open-heart surgery, should this bastion of maleness still exist? Drop in on your typical backyard patio or country fair and you'll find the women dishing up potato salad and cherry pie while the men, armed with long-handled tongs and burger flippers, stand guard at the grill.

Did a guy invent fire? I doubt it. I think a woman invented fire. She was probably sitting around one day thinking how nice it would be to have *steamed* dandelions for a change when the thermodynamic logic of it all just presented itself. Friction. Heat. Oxygen. Combustion. Flame. Presto! Simple, really. So she rubbed a couple of sticks together and organized a cookout.

It was a powerful thing, fire. It brought people together for warmth and fellowship and a good home-cooked meal. It led to the production of more sophisticated tools. And it kept the mosquitoes at bay.

It would also have been an impressive status symbol, a measure of man's skill in the hunt. *Did you see the size of Trog's fire? He must've bagged a big one!* It was certainly far too powerful a symbol to abdicate to the womenfolk. So he took over. And she, having more pressing things to attend to, would have happily acquiesced.

On the other hand, maybe it's the meat itself that stakes out this territory as the male's domain—meat being still, in the eyes of some, the macho component of the meal. *Man kill. Man cook. Man not do tabouleh.* It's the old role-model thing. The famous Argentinian spit-barbecue tradition, the *asado criollo,* originated with the gauchos, the Marlboro Men of the great South American plains. They ranged about the vast grasslands tending their cattle, and when they felt a bit peckish they'd kill one, cook it on a spit and eat it.

The modern-day urban gaucho is spared the bother of roping his next meal. And the open fire has been replaced by a portable, push-button facsimile. But these are minor refinements on an age-old imperative.

Another ceremonial donning-of-the-aprons takes place every January. Again, it appears to be a peculiarly male thing, but the lure this time is not fire or animal flesh but the long-awaited arrival of the season's first Seville oranges. January is the time to make marmalade.

Nobody seems to know what triggers this man-and-his-marmalade phenomenon. Or what proportion of the male population is affected. *The Oxford Companion to Food* mentions it only in passing: "Among all the numerous culinary operations carried out in British domestic kitchens, marmalade-making is one which is quite often performed by men." The author, Alan Davidson, does not venture a guess as to why this should be, why men should be seduced by the marmalade process and not mustard pickles or mango chutney or gooseberry jam. I broached the subject with my own born-in-Britain resident marmalade maker.

"How do you explain this men-in-the-kitchen-with-marmalade thing?" I asked.

He said it was obvious. "If you're British, marmalade is in your genes."

Well, that's a thought. A marmalade gene. That could explain everything—the yearly migration kitchenward, the compulsive rounding up of Mason jars, the seductive come-hither scent of citrus and sugar . . . maybe marmalade making is the expression of some murky, lurky deep-seated mating ritual. Maybe we females should pay more attention.

On the other hand, it could be a simple matter of survival. The supply of that dark, thick-chip Oxford-style staple so lovingly conserved last January has dwindled to a jar or two. Man needs the security of knowing that another year's worth of toast will have adequate coverage. There's always Smuckers, of course. But maybe real men don't eat Smuckers.

Unfortunately, as closer scrutiny revealed, this marmalade-in-the-genes theory is not borne out by the facts. The reality is that from the time marmalade was introduced to the Western world women have been firmly in charge of the whole sticky business.

Take, for example, one of the most famous names in marmalade history: Keiller. The Keiller male, John, was a grocer who lived in Dundee around the end of the eighteenth century. Janet, his wife, helped out in the store. But when a wild storm drove a shipload of Seville oranges off course and into Dundee harbour, it was Janet who seized the moment, purchased the entire cargo of orphaned oranges and, with the sugar stock from the store, turned it into marmalade. It was an instant hit in Dundee, and by 1797 a serendipitous experiment had become a thriving business. But it was Janet's initiative, Janet's recipe, Janet's labour that got the ball rolling.

Frank Cooper's story is similar. He too was a grocer. And it was his wife, Sarah Jane, who, in 1874, using her mom's recipe, created the coarse-cut, aromatic marmalade that quickly caught on amongst the dons and undergraduates of Oxford.

James Robertson, yet another grocer, got into the marmalade trade by default as well. It was his wife, Marion, who boiled up the first batch of Golden Shred in 1864.

So it's curious, isn't it, that what was historically a female initiative should, over time, have become a preoccupation of males?

Nothing I read shed any light on this puzzle. I did, however, find out how marmalade got its name. It derives from the Portuguese word for quince—*marmelo*—an apple-like fruit that, when preserved in unfermented wine and honey, was called *marmelado*. Until well into the eighteenth century, British marmalade was still being made in the "Portugall fashion"—with quinces, and very little liquid. This produced a brick-like, intensely flavoured confection that served as neither a spread nor a breakfast food. A block of marmalade would be sliced and offered up at the end of a meal as a sweetmeat. And a medicine. In 1541, Sir Thomas Elyot in *The Castel of Helth,* suggested that marmalade "mollifyeth the belly" when "abundantly taken" after meat.

It was the Scots who first succeeded in making marmalade spreadable. And the Scots who first thought to spread it on toasted bread at breakfast time. It was still quite thick and sticky though, and the remedy at the time was to thin it further by adding a bit of apple jelly or a splash of tea.

Happily, our house marmalade doesn't need to be sliced. Or thinned with tea. And on marmalade-making day there will be, as always, two cooks in the kitchen. One will be following in the footsteps of the famous marmalade doyennes in history. The other half of the team, the one with the marmalade gene, will compete for jars and lids and counter space to do what a guy's got to do.

No Sex Please, We're Eating

There are things you should know about lettuce, things your mother probably didn't tell you. But you're grown up now and deserve to have the facts: lettuce has a secret life. It's been party to all sorts of shadowy goings-on. This may surprise you. It did me. After all, lettuce looks innocent enough. It's fat free, vitamin rich and, for the most part, green— the colour of choice at smart dinner tables everywhere. It's also Health Canada approved. At least it was. That could change.

For instance, there's the sex thing. Lettuce and sex go back a long way. I know, this is not an association that readily springs to mind as you toss the salad for a family meal. But it's all to do with the shape, you see. For centuries medicinal properties were assigned to plants according to their appearance: lung-shaped leaves were used to treat bronchial problems; the lobed and furrowed configuration of the walnut indicated its healing properties for "fevers of the brain." And the same is true for lettuce, which, in ancient times, was often tall and upright, its leaves flattened around a sturdy central stem. It looked . . . well, it looked very manly. So it was eaten to very manly purpose.

However, if you were required to curb your lustful appetites, if you were holed up in some monastery, say, where upthrusting greenery was deemed inappropriate, you would be obliged to switch lettuces. And there was one popular fallback for that eventuality: a squat variety with stubby roots, which Pythagoras called "eunuch." And, as Margaret Visser points out in *Much Depends on Dinner,* the literal meaning of *eunuch* is "keeping seductive women under control."

On the other hand, if a chap did find himself face to face with a plate of limp eunuch leaves, he could counter any performance-altering side effects with the addition of such traditional pick-me-ups as cress and arugula and mustard. Real men don't eat stubby lettuce. That's the long and the short of it.

Moving right along now from sex to yet another juicy sideline in the secret life of the lettuce: drugs. It seems that lettuce sap, a milky liquid called *lactucarium,* contains a narcotic similar to opium. It's a painkiller and was frequently given to patients before surgery. It's also soporific, which suggests that if you're having a sleepless night you'd be well advised to head straight to the fridge and fix yourself a salad. All this was news to me. I certainly didn't know that lettuce had sap. But in fact the word *lettuce* comes from the Latin *lactua,* a derivative of *lactus,* meaning "milk."

All things considered, you're probably going to want to examine your lettuce more closely and think hard about when and to whom to serve it. You know, check its shape, inspect it for drugs, decide if it's worth the risk. And if the coast is clear and you're looking for serving suggestions I refer you to Aristoxenus, a fourth-century BC Greek of the hedonist persuasion, who had his own ideas about how to dress a lettuce.

Aristoxenus was a foodie of the first order. He was so fanatical he used to wrap his tongue in a little "tongue-bag" to protect its sensitive taste buds between workouts. And he was equally persnickety about the food his tongue encountered, lettuce in particular. He would go to his garden in the evening and sprinkle his lettuce with oil and vinegar while it was still in the ground. He then picked his salad, fully dressed, the next day.

Much depends on the relationship you're in, of course, and the libidos involved, but personally I'd be leery of the Aristoxenus method. I suspect the lettuce would wilt. And wilted lettuce, as we now know, does not augur well for the evening ahead.

Depending on the season, you could well be harbouring yet another titillating veggie along with that sexually suggestive lettuce: asparagus. I love asparagus. And now I know why.

Its allure is as old as time. It grew wild and abundantly in the ancient world. It also grew very big, some spears weighing in at well over half a pound. But long after extreme asparagus fell from fashion, man's passion for this provocatively proportioned vegetable remained at a steady boil. Warning calls resound throughout the ages. *Beware!* they intone. *Asparagus excites lechery! Asparagus manifestly provoketh Venus!* Needless to say, consumption of asparagus soared.

However, despite its relative accessibility, asparagus, like so many good things, gravitated to the tables of the rich. Julius Caesar adored it lightly steamed with lots of melted butter. Marie Antoinette gorged herself shamelessly. Louis XIV was so besotted that his gardener created asparagus beds that could cater to the tastes of Le Roi Soleil all year round. And in nineteenth-century France it was customary

183

for a groom to be served three courses of asparagus on the eve of his wedding. Unfortunately, the effectiveness of this garden-variety Viagra has never been documented.

And while we're here, poking around in this hothouse we call a refrigerator, check out the ginger. There are any number of ways to put fresh ginger to good use. Like—you guessed it—sex. Ginger not only makes it happen, it makes it great. At least that's what they say.

Ages ago, Dioscorides, the "Surgeon General" of Roman times, recognized ginger's stimulative effect on blood circulation. Its energizing heat, it seems, not only improves digestion but lends vitality to other bodily functions as well. Eat ginger in your dotage and, according to the ancients, "you will love and be loved as in your youth."

Once again I am unable to confirm or deny the veracity of this hand-me-down wisdom. I'm working on it, though, drinking lots of ginger tea, steeped with lemon, cinnamon and a cardamom pod or two. Ginger warms. Your cheeks glow, those little knots in your shoulders unravel, and your toes curl up with the pleasure of it all. Then, I can confidently report, you fall asleep.

Never mind. There are, as I say, other useful things to do with ginger.

It makes an excellent tiger repellant, for one thing. At least that's the opinion of a Frenchman named Dr. Fallet, whose credentials I'm unable to vouch for but whose theory I think must be sound. We keep three kinds of ginger in the house—pickled, powdered and fresh—and though we've been pestered by ants, spiders, tent caterpillars and gangs of feral cats, we have never, ever been harassed by tigers.

Then there's the ginger suppository, a very popular item with the horsey set. Carefully positioned and gingerly applied, it will send even the most decrepit of nags into a giddy prance, her tail held jauntily aloft like a filly in springtime. You have only to put yourself in the horse's shoes for the briefest moment to see that this would work.

One very helpful suggestion comes, via *The Ginger Book* by Stephen Fulder, from the natives of Papua New Guinea. It's one of those when-it-absolutely-positively-has-to-get-there courier things. It seems that the natives would ensure the safe delivery of a canoe-load of special cargo by chewing on ginger and spitting on the package in question. I assume it works because I know too well what happens when you *don't* spit on your mail. Last year we sent an unsullied, 100 percent spittle-free Christmas parcel to Toronto on December 2 and it didn't arrive until the week after New Year's. We'll be taking appropriate measures to expedite delivery next time.

Another useful thing to know about ginger is that it smothers burps and diffuses other gassy eruptions that can wreak such havoc in confined spaces. Queen Elizabeth I had a special ginger-laced "pother" (powder) that was passed among her guests to forestall any embarrassing passing of "winde" in the royal presence. You could try this, when the wind gets up, at your next dinner party.

Which brings us to the dessert course: chocolate. Another scoop and—brace yourself— more unsettling news of licentious goings-on in unexpected places. Please note: what I am about to reveal must be treated with the utmost discretion. In fact, just as a precaution, I suggest that after you've read these pages you wad them up into a bite-size ball and swallow it. Don't worry about intestinal complications. Spies eat incriminating bits of paper all the time.

The point is, this is highly sensitive material and the Authorities are not going to like it one bit. The Authorities being that gang of busybodies who decide, on our behalf, just how much of a good thing is too much of a good thing, then slap a tax on it. Or outlaw it altogether.

The fact is that the news about chocolate, as far as you and I are concerned, is very encouraging. Calorie engorged and nutritionally challenged as it may be, chocolate is actually *good for you.* Good for you in pharmacological terms, that is, as a sensory enhancer and a mood-altering stimulant. In other words, chocolate is a lot like dope.

The stimulative effects of chocolate have long been recognized. Substances such as theobromine and caffeine, which are found in the cacao bean, zap our heart, muscles and brain. But that's old news. There's another group of compounds in chocolate that affects the same areas of the brain in the same ways as cannabis; they diminish feelings of anxiety, heighten our awareness of all things sensory and induce a mood of unbridled happiness. Which is, of course, exactly what the Authorities want to protect us from. We all know how dangerous unbridled happiness can be.

Then there's phenylethylamine, or PEA, which works on our bodies in much the same way as amphetamines do. The bonus is that in chocolate, PEA combines with salsolinol, an antidepressant, to boost our happiness quotient to even giddier heights.

And as if that weren't enough good news for one day, it seems that there just might be some truth to a theory that has been bandied about for some five hundred years: chocolate is a powerful aphrodisiac. I know, I know. The choco-skeptics among us will be quick to point out that just about every food, from oysters to tiger's whiskers, has been labelled a love potion at one time or another. But this is *chocolate*, for heaven's sake! It's worth a try. Share a Mars bar with someone you fancy and see what develops.

Happiness, if nothing else, is guaranteed. And the best part is that that lovely, buzzy PEA high is available, without a prescription, at a store near you.

Auntie Lynn's Little Pots de Chocolat

An exquisite offering of life-enhancing chocolate from the dear friend—and designated "auntie" to my three sons—who shared it with me.

7 ounces top-quality semisweet chocolate (No substitutes. Chocolate-on-the-cheap will not do.)
1 cup heavy cream
1 egg
1 tablespoon brandy or rum

Break up the chocolate and chop it in a food processor. Bring the cream to a boil over medium heat, add it to the chocolate and whiz it around until well blended. Add the egg along with the rum or brandy and process it, briefly, again. Pour the mixture into 6 small ramekins and refrigerate at least 2 hours.

That's it. Six tiny, perfect examples of decadence made easy.

Food and sex have been inextricably linked throughout the ages, sometimes in the most puzzling ways. Take the Italian pasta dish called puttanesca, for example. The recipe varies but the story behind it does not. It's a story that requires some discretion in the telling, dealing, as it does, with what is delicately referred to as "mature subject matter."

Pasta Puttanesca takes its name from *puttane,* the Italian word for women with highly specialized skills who earn their livelihood in the "personal service" sector of the workplace. Their job is a competitive and physically demanding one. Long hours and the invariable ups and downs of a touch-and-go lifestyle afford the busy professional little opportunity for homey diversions like menu planning. Slow-simmered pot roast and stuffed mushroom caps are unlikely options. She's got other things on her plate.

The two versions of this dish I am most familiar with are from *The Silver Palate* by Julee Rosso and Sheila Lukins, and Giuliano Bugialli's book *The Fine Art of Italian Cooking.* I can find no reference to it in Waverley Root's comprehensive study of Italian cuisine. My decades-old copy of *Joy of Cooking* avoids the subject entirely. And though it occurred to me that the *puttane* themselves, in the tradition of other women's service groups, might have published their own collection of personal favourites, I failed to track one down.

Bugialli's version calls for piping-hot pasta topped with a sauce made from fresh tomatoes, garlic, olive oil and basil. The sauce is uncooked and served cold. In fact, Bugialli is adamant that in order to release the "unforgettable flavours" of this dish the sauce should be very, very cold and the pasta very, very hot. I'm not sure what to read into this, and if Bugialli knows, he isn't saying.

The version presented in *The Silver Palate* is a tad more labour intensive, though it too can be ready to eat with about twenty minutes' notice. It's spicier. In fact it's quite audacious in its aggressive collision of powerful tastes. It too has a tomato base, enlivened in this case with anchovies, capers, garlic, hot peppers and oregano.

Which is the genuine article? And why? Both versions are cheap and tasty and easy to make, ideal for the busy professional with lusty appetites and a jam-packed calendar. One delivers, delicately accented, the ripe tastes of summer in all its lushness. The other captures the robust flavours and aromas of the peasant's palate. Both, I noted, call for garlic, and lots of it. Was this a way of hastening each transaction to a speedy conclusion? Or did the heady drift of garlic lend an earthy edge to the business at hand?

I don't have the answer to this. Both my sources are coyly evasive as to the reasons behind the dish's provocative name. And if a quick bite were all that a working girl required, surely a pot of mac and cheese or a slice of pizza would do the trick. So to speak.

I consulted the list of aphrodisiacs that I keep for ready

reference should the occasion arise. Frogs. Shark fin. Hyena eyes. No, there was nothing in this long and improbable compendium of stimulants that bore any relevance to the puzzle at hand. Tomatoes got a fleeting mention. As did fish. But this seemed a slim lead and I redirected my investigation along other avenues.

Which of these two options would *I* choose if I were in the *puttana*'s posi . . . er, circumstances? I mulled over this scenario and decided that I'd likely not settle for either. The prospect of a hastily concocted solo meal sandwiched between business appointments seemed shabby and inadequate recompense indeed. Given my druthers, I wouldn't cook at all. I would insist on eating out. In style. Preferably in an establishment where the ladies' menu posted no prices. And I'd eat whatever took my fancy—steamed lobster with drawn butter, perhaps, or a plump grilled squab, accompanied by lots of robust red wine and good conversation. That would be part of the deal. No mucking about over a two-burner hot plate for me.

I realize of course that business opportunities could be somewhat compromised as a result. Prospective clients would have to pass a means test before any transaction could be considered. My roundish figure, already well past its best-before date, would undoubtedly assume proportions out of keeping with the standards of the trade. And besides, all that eating and drinking would necessitate long, and preferably solitary, post-prandial naps. And naps mean downtime, without pay.

I decided I was not really cut out for this kind of work. I

also decided that what other professional women choose to cook and eat, for whatever reasons, was no business of mine. However, I still rustle up a spicy puttanesca from time to time. Puttanesca for two, which is the way I like it best.

7

Desperate Measures

Even an old boot tastes good
if it is cooked over charcoal.

ITALIAN FOLK SAYING

Catch as Catch Can

There's an entire school of cookery based on meals born out of desperation, in crisis conditions, fashioned from whatever happens to be lying around at the time.

One of the best-known examples is chicken Marengo, a dish created for Napoleon by a French chef named Dunand on June 14, 1800. And there's the less-famous but equally impressive quail *Exxon Valdez*, which was assembled in recent times from an improbable collection of odds and ends on Galiano Island, British Columbia.

Dunand's chicken dish emerged from the heat of battle. Napoleon had defeated the Austrians in a showdown near Marengo, in Piedmont, and had pursued the fleeing enemy with such vigour that much of his company was left far behind. Dunand, to his credit, had managed to stay the course. The commissary, with the army's entire supply of food, did not.

It seems that Napoleon made it a practice never to eat before going into battle. So, with the enemy dispersed and the dust of battle finally settled, he turned his attention to his rumbling tummy and demanded to be fed.

Dunand was in a spot. Without so much as a bean or a pot to put it in, he dispatched a handful of soldiers into the countryside to forage for a meal. They returned with the following: one chicken, four tomatoes, three eggs, half a dozen crayfish, garlic and some olive oil. They also managed to track down a frying pan—at least this is what the history books tell us. Maybe Piedmont is famous for its wild frying pans. Anyway, luck was with them. And Dunand made do.

He cut up the bird and fried it in the oil and garlic, adding a little water, which he fortified with some cognac filched, it is said, from Napoleon's own canteen.

He bulked up this impromptu fry-up with a ration of bread donated by one of the soldiers and set the eggs to bubbling on the side. Then—evidence of the beleaguered chef's desperate frame of mind—he placed the crayfish on top of the whole seething mess to steam.

Napoleon was delighted. In fact, so taken was he with Dunand's invention that he ordered it be served to him after every battle from that day on.

Horrified, Dunand set about to rescue the dish and, not incidentally, his reputation. He substituted white wine for the water, added some wild mushrooms, eliminated the crayfish and presented this new, improved version to his boss. Napoleon, as it turns out, was a very superstitious man.

"You left out the crayfish," he told Dunand angrily. "You will bring me bad luck." The crayfish were reluctantly reinstated.

Today, most French chefs omit this fishy refinement, but not in Piedmont, where the tradition remains intact and chicken Marengo comes complete with crayfish, croutons (symbolic of the soldier's ration of bread) and fried eggs on the side.

A more recent example of quick-thinking-in-a-culinary-pinch is one involving, among other found things, oil. Rather a lot of oil. Which is why it has become known as quail *Exxon Valdez*. The enterprising chef in this instance was my husband. The challenge was the care and feeding of a hungry woman—me—returning home from a day of road rage and bad burgers in the city. There was, as far as he could tell, next to nothing to eat in the entire house. The thought crossed his mind that with any luck at all I'd have snacked en route, filled the gaps with a tub or two of B.C. Ferries' coleslaw, which, he knows, I am very partial to. But no. I arrived home hungry. And like Napoleon, wanted to be fed.

Undaunted, the chef, like Dunand before him, went instantly into foraging mode, and from the clutter in the fridge and a larder well stocked with Miss Mew and little else, he extracted the following: one good-size potato; two oranges; a stub end of gingerroot; soy sauce; a wedge of limp leftover pizza; a small Bibb lettuce, a few rag-tag bits of spinach, several quarts of olive oil and—miracle of miracles!—two half-frozen quail.

You're wondering about the quail. The chef certainly did. How did two exotic birds find their way into our fridge with neither of us noticing? It's a fair question. But I can explain. They were an impulse purchase. I'd dashed to the store for some essential or other—lime juice, as I recall—and there they were. I'd meant to pop them in the freezer and forgot. These things happen. Especially when you've got other things on your mind. Like margaritas. Besides, the chef was grateful for the lapse. We had the beginnings of a meal.

The pizza, heated up and judiciously apportioned, would make serviceable bite-size hors d'oeuvres. The greens, refreshed and lightly dressed, made for a legitimate, if somewhat minimalist, salad. But the quails were more problematic. They were the size of marginally overweight hummingbirds. Anyone else would have popped them in the toaster and served them up as finger food. But this was a crisis of larger proportions and toasted quail tidbits were not an option. So, drawing inspiration from a Chinese recipe for *yashao ya* (oil-braised duck), the chef set to work.

The tiny birds were simmered in an aromatic broth of orange juice, soy sauce and ginger, then plunged into hot oil to crisp. They were then towelled down, bathed in a satiny reduction of the orange-ginger sauce and served, fusion style, on nests of perfect golden frites.

It was a marvellous meal, all things considered. It was also a history-making one because *Exxon Valdez*–style oil-drenched quail is not likely to be reproduced any time soon. The chef was adamant on that point.

"Too much stress," he said, reaching for the wine bottle. "It gives a whole new meaning to the term 'pressure-cooker.'"

Necessity, they say, is the mother of invention. It is also closely related to that old standby, the reasonable facsimile. I found this out the day I decided that come hell or high water, I had to have a bouillabaisse. The last time I'd felt a need this urgent I was hugely pregnant and absolutely convinced that without an instant infusion of several pounds of Bing cherries I'd not make it through the night. I got my cherries. And a few weeks later I delivered a healthy, vitamin-enriched, nine-and-a-half-pound baby boy.

Bouillabaisse is a fisherman's stew that originated in Marseille. I found a recipe in a tattered old book by M. Reboul, *La Cuisinière Provençale*. It's at least a century old. Its pages are yellow. And it is written in French.

It begins by pointing out the folly of making the dish for fewer than eight people. I could see why. The recipe calls for eleven kinds of fish. I invited two friends to join us, warning them that although bouillabaisse was what I was aiming for bouillabaisse was not necessarily what they'd get. But not to worry, I assured them. Whatever transpired, there would be lots.

The big challenge was the fish list: oddities such as crawfish, rascasse, gurnet, roucaou, John Dory, monkfish, whiting and conger eel. Needless to say, a quick search of the freezer turned up none of the above. Besides, half of them were unpronounceable and the rest I'd never heard of. Like gurnet, or gurnard, which is known as sea robin in North America. It swims close to the surface making low croaking noises, so I'd likely know one if I met one but I never have. John Dory is a European species, unlikely to be encountered here. Rascasse is a spiny red fish found only in Mediterranean waters. And the conger eel, I found out, is a saltwater monster. It can reach ten feet in length and weigh as much as 170 pounds.

I did, however, find a can of baby clams in the cupboard. And an emergency run to a neighbourhood store netted me a rigid slab of frozen lingcod and one halibut fillet. Reasonable enough substitutes, I figured, circumstances being what they were.

Having strayed so far from the original by now, I consulted other recipes hoping for a more forgiving approach to this mission of mine. *Joy of Cooking*, humbly acknowledging the Americanization of this Provençal classic, suggested clams and mussels. Well, I had a can of one and none of the other and besides, *Larousse* was vehement that, under no circumstances, should a mollusc of any description find its way into a traditional bouillabaisse. I abandoned *Larousse* and pressed on.

Leeks, onions, garlic I had. A sliver of orange peel? No oranges. Lemon would have to do. James Beard suggested lobster. I wish. I did, however, find a jar of pickled herring, but, keeping a cool head, rejected that. A splash of Pernod? No Pernod. Pity. I settled for vodka instead and poured myself a consolatory tipple.

There were two ingredients—aside from fish, of course—that appeared to be non-negotiable: fennel and saffron. This was the break I was looking for. I could probably get away with fennel seeds. And, to my great delight, buried in the fragrant chaos of my spice drawer was a jewel-box-size container with a few shrivelled threads of saffron inside. Wonderful!

I know that what follows is a travesty. I feel badly, as if I'd been caught slopping ketchup on caviar. But I make no apologies. My go-with-the-flow bouillabaisse was worlds removed from Reboul's authentic fish stew of Marseilles. But it was amazingly good nonetheless. We lapped it up and wished for more.

My Own Fool-Ya Bouillabaisse

¼ cup extra-virgin olive oil

4 cloves garlic, minced

2 leeks, white part only, thinly sliced

½ onion, chopped

1 teaspoon fennel seeds

1 teaspoon minced lemon zest

6 (or more) saffron threads

¼ teaspoon sambal oelek (or a pinch of chili flakes)

1 teaspoon sea salt

Freshly ground pepper

28-ounce can tomatoes, chopped, with their juice

7-ounce can baby clams, with broth

2 pounds fish (a combination of halibut and cod), cut into
  bite-size pieces

¼ cup vodka

Heat the olive oil in a large, heavy saucepan over medium heat. Add the garlic, leeks, onion, fennel seeds, lemon zest, saffron, sambal oelek, salt and pepper. Cook for a few minutes until everything smells great and the leeks and onions are just soft. Add the tomatoes and their juice and the clam broth (not the clams yet) and let this simmer gently for 15 minutes.

Add the fish, the clams, the vodka and enough hot water,

if needed, to cover the fish. Boil briskly for 7 or 8 minutes until the fish is cooked through. Serve at once.

Serves 4.

Dinner by Candlelight Again?

We often eat by candlelight. In fact, we eat by candlelight more often than not. Which is fine and dandy, deliriously romantic even, if candle power happens to be your power of choice. I'm rather partial to electricity myself, but that's not always available where I live. Because here, when winter winds get up and trees come down, you can be without power for endless dark days at a time.

I used to adore the idea of dinner by candlelight. I'd actually extinguish the lights deliberately in order to eat in the glow of a candle in a Chianti bottle. Now when the lights go out we grit our teeth and move instantly into survival mode, which, from my rather specialized view of the world, focuses single-mindedly on one thing and one thing only. *Food.* What—and how—will we eat?

We have a wood-burning stove that we can press into action at times like this, but it takes a while to get up to speed. In the meantime we need to eat or we're sure to die, so we fumble around under the mitten box on the top shelf of the closet for the camp stove.

A dozen flashlights are strategically positioned around the house for emergencies such as this, but of course we can't find them in the dark. (Speaking of which, have you ever noticed how much darker dark is when it isn't your idea?) What we need are candles. We have candles, lots of them, and I know exactly where they are, but, visibility being what it is, I walk straight into the dog's water dish and we now have a small lake to portage in order to get to them.

We decide on soup for supper. Soup from a can is the easy thing but that's something we rarely have on hand because soup's something you make from scratch if you're a true-grit Harrowsmith-style islander. Happily, someone has seen fit to cheat. We've got a shortcut: a packet of Macayama Senegalese instant soup. Good. Now all we need is water. During the Blizzard of '96 we tried melting snow only to discover that it takes approximately 60 cubic feet of the stuff (half a deck-load) to melt down to two cups of water. These days we keep a lineup of full pails at the ready, attractively arranged near sinks and toilets and in various nooks and crannies around the house.

Supper is soup, bread and butter, a bottle of wine and bright smiles all round. We are so *lucky*, we tell ourselves. Just think of being in this pickle without a bottle of wine!

We discuss the advisability of calling BC Hydro for an update. We've called once. Twice could be construed as nagging and we don't want to appear like wimps, like we can't manage these minor blips in our pampered lives.

The Power Is Yours, says the ad campaign. Oh, really? It occurs to me that *The Power Is On* might be more reassuring.

After our candlelight dinner we leave the washing up for the dog to do and settle down in front of the fire to read. There's nothing on TV.

We have twelve candles stuffed into twelve beer bottles on the table between us. The light, perfect for dreaming by, is less than ideal for a long night with a good book. I follow Inspector Morse's comings and goings by flashlight. Chris has one of those mini-headlamps. It's for managing close-up manoeuvres in his woodworking shop but he uses it more and more these days for simply getting around.

The house is quite cold by now, so we stay by the fire eating Jelly Bellys and avoiding bed. The sheets, when we finally slither, gasping, between them, are like two thin skins of ice, the warmth of our electric blanket little more than a distant memory.

Breakfast—we are still powerless—is another catch-as-catch-can-in-the-dark affair. Coffee is in bean form, chewable but otherwise unusable. The orange juice is warm—it's been in the fridge all night, after all—so we fire up the wood-stove, settle for bread and marmalade, and wait for the water to boil for tea. Nothing wrong with tea, I suppose, unless your entire day rides on a hit of high-test Sumatra-style caffeine. Which mine does.

I sip tea and watch the wind rock the trees. There's a warm dog at my feet and a cat in my lap and enough light, for a while at least, to read by. Things could be worse, I decide. I could be stuck on some remote beach somewhere with a string of plastic bananas around my neck. And sand in my piña colada.

I'm Eating as Fast as I Can

With winter's bluster behind us, the gentle hand of summer should, by rights, usher in a season of domestic calm. This is not the case. Summer, in my culinary world, is a time of high anxiety. This is the season of plenty. The season of too much to eat.

Market stalls are heaped with all things irresistible, a feast of freshness the likes of which we'll not see again for another year. I want it all: cherries, raspberries, peaches, pears and plums; cauliflower, cucumbers, onions, carrots, lettuces in various shapes and colours and, because they're there, zucchini. My fridge begins to buckle and wheeze under the load. My freezer's still stuffed with last summer's stockpile. And I'm eating as fast as I can.

At breakfast I tackle the fruit, eating it by the bowl-load, or buzzing it with yogurt in a blender and drinking it. There is still plenty left for many breakfasts to come. I broach the veggies at lunch: a salad for two that, in the grand tradition of loaves and fishes, becomes a salad for six. I now have salad leftovers and several bushels of virgin veggies waiting in the wings.

Dinnertime. I make ratatouille. This has to be a radically modified, zucchini-heavy ratatouille, as I have no eggplant and have resisted, wisely, the temptation to buy one. I compensate with plenty of onions, slip in some cauliflower and, once again, I overshoot. We now have ratatouille *and* salad leftovers along with all the other stuff waiting to be turned into leftovers. I hang a No Vacancy sign on the fridge and hunker down to plan our next meal.

How do I get myself in these pickles anyway? It's my problem, I know. But it's not my fault. What we've got here is production mismanagement of major proportions. Huge overruns exacerbated by extreme consumer fatigue. And who's minding the shop? Mother Nature, that's who. She's in charge. And she's run amuck.

Mother Nature doesn't give a fig that you ache for a bowl of fresh raspberries in January. Raspberries, it is decreed, will be served for two weeks only. In July. That's it. This puts your average raspberry fan under intolerable pressure. If you're to get your share you'll have to resort to heroic measures.

Ralph Waldo Emerson once said, "There are only ten minutes in the life of a pear when it is perfect to eat." Which is why pears, like all good things that summer brings, pile up. And why, if my fridge and I are to make it through another season, we'd need professional help.

I really haven't the faintest idea what goes on inside my fridge. And that makes me nervous. Perfectly good food put by for safekeeping morphs into sludge when my back is turned. Summers are particularly unsettling, of course, but my fridge's treachery knows no season. Wieners sprout fur. Cucumbers implode. Plastic tubs of mystery stuff gravitate to shadowy corners and take on a life of their own. And because I know perfectly well I'm not going to like what I find there, I simply ignore it all and hope it self-destructs.

What I need is a fridge management consultant.

I've never met anyone in this line of work so I'm not sure

what to expect. It would have to be someone with a strong stomach and the cool detachment of an undertaker. A pro who can resist the temptation to resuscitate a limp carrot and go fearlessly into those dark and slippery places where no one's gone before.

I've got it all worked out. We'd start with a tour of the freezer section, where the baby peas have escaped their bag and gathered in petrified heaps here, there and everywhere. No problem, not with my guide at my side. We corral the peas and pitch them. Next: something in a yogurt tub buried under a snowdrift. It has a label: *Chicken curry/April 2002*. The expert rolls her eyes. The curry goes. So easy.

What's this? A pale lump in shrink wrap. Pizza dough? A body part? I'll never know. It's garbage.

We're on a roll now. I'm learning as we go. Green ricotta, my consultant explains, is not worth saving. Cat food and rhubarb pie do not good shelf-mates make. My collection of egg whites is past its prime. I should have frozen them, individually, in ice cube trays. (I'd not thought of that. If I were the kind of person who thought up these things we wouldn't be in the mess we're in.) We find the chicken carcass I thought I'd lost behind the Christmas fruitcake. "Bad packing," she says. And those little tubs of mystery stuff? Close examination of their variously coloured, woolly-coated contents tells us nothing. And the only way I am to get past my fear of those scuzzy little tubs is to face them down bravely, pitch where appropriate and devise a better filing system.

Filing is not my forte, I tell her. I forget things. And I'm pathetically inconsistent. Life's a muddle. My fridge is a muddle. Everything's hopeless.

Had I considered feng shui? she asks. I confess I hadn't. We ponder the nuances of spatial harmony, positive energy flow and the optimal positioning of shelves and drawers. Perhaps, she says, if my fridge door faced north instead of south . . . ? I point out that if my fridge faced north the door would be against the wall. I couldn't open it. I couldn't stuff stuff into it. Or get stuff out.

"True," says my fridge management consultant. "So it might be worth considering."

Please Don't Eat the Thistles

The artichoke, according to the English food writer Jane Grigson, is the "vegetable expression of civilized living." I don't really buy that. I think the artichoke is simply an example of biting off more than you can chew.

I've been more than a bit suspicious of this curious and cumbersome vegetable ever since my first exposure many years ago. We were in California and, ready as always for any culinary adventure that came our way, had ordered an artichoke each for appetizers.

Diving in, as is my wont, I had managed to gnaw a sizable swath through a layer or two of rubber-like greenery before the correct choke protocol was pointed out to me.

It was my husband who set me straight, thank goodness.

I'd noticed an anxious-looking waiter hovering nearby, wringing his hands and debating, I'm sure, the wisdom of interceding in what was shaping up to be a very public and decidedly messy suicide attempt.

"Not the whole leaf, dear," my husband cautioned. "Just the meaty bit at the base."

Bracts. They're bracts, not leaves. But I wasn't exactly in a position to lecture.

Although the delicate heart, when I eventually unearthed it, proved an exquisite treat indeed, I was particularly taken with the lemon-infused puddle of butter that accompanied my artichoke. That was good. And, I decided, best taken straight. Because when all was said and done and I was elbow deep in leftovers, I was at a loss to explain why we persist in this complicated ritual. As Lord Chesterfield once said, "The artichoke is the only vegetable of which you have more at the finish that you do at the start."

The truth is that nothing about the artichoke is simple. Even the name has impossibly tangled roots. It has nothing to do with the heart or the choke. It comes from the Arabic *al kharshuf*, meaning "the thistle." *Kharshuf* was then borrowed by the Spanish and evolved to *alcachofa*. It was subsequently reissued in French as *artichaut* and eventually filtered into the English language to become what we know as the *artichoke*.

That's a fair mouthful, I know, which is just as well as it's about the only mouthful you're likely to encounter where artichokes are concerned.

So what's the allure? What is it about the artichoke that

could possibly persuade us to spend the better part of a meal hour bushwhacking through a spiny forest for a taste we can enjoy, fuss free and for pennies apiece, out of a jar?

Maybe it's the artichoke's reputation as an aphrodisiac, although I can't imagine why. By the time you've excavated the edible bit you'll have forgotten why you wanted to get there in the first place.

Maybe it's a minimalist thing: food for people who prefer not to clutter up their lives with food.

Perhaps it's the cachet surrounding anything that smacks of the exotic and unusual. Forget you're eating a thistle. This is a case of ceremony over substance. The elaborate ritual attached to the artichoke's preparation, its special-occasion presentation and the extraordinary pains undertaken in the eating lend it a mystique that separates it from a forkful of parsnips as surely as Dom Perignon stands aloof from Baby Duck.

Whatever the reasons, I'm not likely to be persuaded. I have too short an attention span. When I'm hungry I want to eat something without deconstructing it first. As one anti-artichoke activist once said, "You get as much satisfaction from eating an artichoke as you would from chewing your fingernails."

Annette's Artichoke Dip

This is another celebrated local dish, this time from a friend whose other claim to fame is her infectious laugh. We get together often, just for the fun of it, and I always ask her to bring her dip. I am grateful to her for discovering something useful to do with artichokes.

2 (6-ounce) jars marinated artichokes, drained
6 tablespoons freshly grated Parmesan cheese
4 tablespoons mayonnaise (*Good* mayonnaise. Annette
  uses Hellman's)
3 to 4 cloves garlic, crushed
Dash of fresh lemon juice
Salt and pepper to taste

Preheat oven to 375°F.

Put all the ingredients in a food processor and blend well. Adjust seasonings to taste. Put mixture in an oven-proof casserole and bake until it's heated through, about 20 minutes.

Serve warm with crudités, pita bread or any dippable edible you can get your hands on. Remember to share.

Makes 1½ cups of dip.

I Think I'm Going to Be Sick

There's nothing wrong with
a little drink from time to time.
As long as it isn't water.

J. WALKER

Oddly enough, the word *hangover* does not appear in the *Oxford English Dictionary*. This curious omission suggests one of two things: either people didn't get hangovers prior to 1971 (which is when my particular edition came out), or the compilers of dictionaries don't go to the same parties I do.

I should point out that I had not gone to the dictionary to look up *hangover*. I know perfectly well what a hangover is. I was looking up *hartshorn*. I'd heard somewhere that hartshorn is a restorative made from antler shavings and used to combat faintness and headache. It sounded promising. There wasn't an aspirin in the house, so the idea of a restorative on this particular morning was very much top of mind.

But without a ready supply of antlers and a steady hand at the razor, where does one turn? We can clone sheep. We can grow watermelons without seeds. We can make dolls that snore when you tuck them into bed. But science has not, as far as I know, come up with a cure for the hangover.

So here are some do-it-yourself remedies I've compiled, at great personal cost, over the years.

212

First of all, it's important to establish that what you've got is in fact a hangover and not the early symptoms of chicken flu. Here is a simple test that you can do at home: stand on one leg to put your sock on. If you topple over you've got chicken flu. If you can't remember why you're standing there in the dim half light with a sock in your hand, you've got a hangover.

The remedies I'm most familiar with date from my college days, and for these credit must go to the trio of tireless hosts of many a five-day-weekend party—"the Three Roomies," namely Freeps, Burnsy and Pork. (Their real names are subject to a publication ban, which is unlikely to be lifted this century.)

The Three Roomies were quartered in a mildewed apartment complex called the Betty Ann. They are best remembered for a lethal purple punch concocted in, and served from, an old claw-foot bathtub. But, ever attentive, they did not simply dispense the poison. They were there to administer the morning-after antidote as well. Here are two of their best.

The Three Roomies' Bull Shot

2 ounces vodka

4 ounces beef bouillon

Small splash of Worcestershire sauce

Pinch of salt

Dribble of lemon juice

As much cayenne pepper as you can stand

Stir it all together. Serve over ice with a slice of lemon.

The Betty Ann Red-Eye
Beer and tomato juice.

That's it. The proportions depend entirely upon the state of one's functioning organs at the time.

My favourite food writer, M. F. K. Fisher, recommends a Prairie Oyster: "One fresh raw unbeaten egg, one douse of Worcestershire sauce, one souse of whiskey or brandy, and one optional dibble of Tabasco . . . in that order of hell-fire progression."

If you suspect that a raw egg might not stay put long enough to be effective, you could try Ms. Fisher's back-up remedy: a nourishing bowl of gazpacho soup, liberally laced with Tabasco.

Hot peppers and alcohol. These were recurrent themes in many of the cures I came across.

Cayenne pepper, *Capsicum annuum,* has some impressive credentials in this area. It is loaded with vitamins C and A and has been used for years by herbalists to treat all manner of ailments from asthma to toothaches. But of particular relevance to our current pursuit is its high concentration of a substance called capsaicin, which both stimulates and soothes those parts of the body we have so capriciously abused.

It is, according to herbalist Maude Grieve, a superb medicine "for purging the system of bad humours." And goodness knows, bad humour's what we're dealing with here.

And alcohol? Well, it's the old hair-of-the-dog approach: get your hands on a hair of the dog that bit you and you won't get rabies. I've never tested the rabies-prevention theory. But, like millions before me, I have, on the odd occasion, bought into its dibble-of-brandy corollary.

However, if you're not up to broaching the bottle for your morning-after cure there are dozens of nonalcoholic suggestions to help you face the day. Like turkey vegetable soup with—you guessed it—lots of Tabasco. You could try downing a jug of ice-cold Gatorade. Or Welch's grape juice. Some swear by a combination of V8 juice served, with a clove of crushed garlic and one jalapeño pepper, over ice. And I have it on good authority that Flintstones ice-pops work miracles.

Here's one for when all else fails: stand in the middle of the room (the place where you left the sock that flummoxed you earlier) and wave your arms around, making big windmill-like circles in the air. This apparently encourages the blood to flow to those areas of the brain most critically affected.

The important thing is to give your body a chance to acclimatize itself to all this unaccustomed attention. It will be confused. Messages from the brain will be lost or rerouted in all kinds of disorienting ways. But give it time. My best advice is to crawl under a duvet with a fistful of hot peppers and don't come out till the next party.

A Tax Dodger's Menu Plan

When I think of salad I think of fresh greens tossed in a pretty bowl with a splash of vinegar and good olive oil. Or late-summer tomatoes with basil and bocconcini. I think of potato salads, Caesar salads, fruit salads and coleslaw. There are onion and orange salads. And salads suspended in neon-bright Jell-O. Sometimes salads are warm, but mostly they're cold.

The point is, you'd probably know one when you saw one. You're not likely to confuse a salad with a plate of chopped liver. Or a tub of fries. Or are you?

The question is not as silly as you might think because, believe it or not, there does seem to be some confusion out there. And by "out there" I mean way out there, beyond the point where reason resides and real life has any relevance: Ottawa, our nation's capital and home of the *GST News*.

GST stands for goods and services tax, which imposes a levy of 7 percent on the cost of just about everything we Canadians buy, from cars and shoes and bread machines to sushi lunches and realtors' fees. Canadians hate the GST. The *GST News*, on the other hand, which at one time was published quarterly by Revenue Canada, is a source of hilarity and delight to its readers. And it's proven to be a goldmine for collectors of nonsense like me: items like how to meet your GST obligations; returnable beverage container tax allocation protocol; and a most imaginative piece on the tax status of salads. Or, more specifically, how to determine what a salad actually is in order to slap a tax on it.

This is the definition of salad that Revenue Canada came up with: "Food containing ingredients, whether mixed or not, such as chopped, shredded, diced, sliced, or puréed vegetables, meat, fish, eggs, or other food when supplied with a dressing and/or seasonings whether or not the dressing is mixed with the other ingredients, is considered to be a salad for purposes of determining its GST status."

Perhaps we should examine this more closely. Or, better still, let's try to re-create the debate that made such a hash of this familiar household commodity.

These guidelines would have been drawn up by a Task Force, a Task Force being a collection of recycled bureaucrats brought together at enormous expense for the purpose of debating the obvious.

Various contenders for salad status would have been presented for adjudication. Some, shredded cabbage and mayo, for example, would be instantly recognizable and promptly categorized: this is definitely what you call a salad. Other food combos would have proven more problematic. Take a wiener, for instance. Chop it up, squirt on some French's mustard, and what have you got? Chopped-up wiener with mustard on it. That's a layperson's view of things. But the gang in Ottawa could see things quite differently.

A wiener, after all, is a *food containing ingredients*, is it not? Add mustard and it is food *accompanied by a dressing and/or seasoning*, right? Ergo, what we have here, folks, is a *wiener salad!*

The same logic could apply to puréed spinach, which, to a simpleton like me, qualifies unreservedly for the designation *puréed spinach*. But there is room for debate here as well. What happens when you squeeze a bit of lemon on your plate of puréed spinach? Only our Task Force knows for sure. They have in front of them a further elaboration on the definition of salad: "A combination of one ingredient and a dressing or seasoning(s) which is sold or represented as a salad, is also considered to be a salad."

Therefore: a puddle of spinach + a dribble of lemon = whatever one deems it to be. Heads it's a salad, tails it's not. The guidelines provide ample latitude in this regard. You could cut a Twinkie into small pieces, serve it up with a drizzle of Kraft Green Goddess dressing and make a convincing argument for chopped Twinkie salad.

You can perhaps begin to appreciate the mind-bending array of possibilities this presents: just about anything with ingredients, in almost any form, when enhanced with a seasoning of almost any kind can be labelled, for the purposes of a tax grab, a salad. Brilliant! Porridge wouldn't qualify, of course, not on its own. But add a dash of soy sauce, or a sprinkling of lemon pepper, maybe even brown sugar, and you've got a salad. You'd have to *call* it a salad, of course, in order for it to be official.

Porridge salad. There. Done. If only real life were that simple.

Recipes for Disaster

Here's a recipe that caught my eye.

Baked Camel (stuffed)

Serves 400

200 plover eggs
20 two-pound carp
500 dates
4 bustards, cleaned and plucked
2 sheep
1 large camel
Seasonings

Dig trench. Light fire. Reduce inferno to hot coals, three feet in depth. Hard-cook eggs. Scale carp and stuff with shelled eggs and dates. Season bustards and stuff with carp. Stuff stuffed bustards into sheep and stuff sheep into camel. Singe camel. Then wrap in leaves of doum palm and bury in pit. Bake two days. Serve with rice.

Perhaps a little background would be helpful. The recipe is from a riotously funny novel called *Water Music*, by

T. Coraghessan Boyle. The hero, Mungo Park—a real-life Scottish explorer—is stumbling through the wilds of Western Africa tracing the course of the Niger. The dish described is the pièce de resistance at a wedding feast recorded by Mungo during a lengthy and involuntary stopover at an encampment of bad-tempered, well-armed Moors.

What delighted me about this particular dish—apart from the ingredient list—was the babushka-style space-saving ingenuity that delivers an entire banquet to a large crowd without messing up a whole lot of pots and pans. Imagine the yelps of pleasure as your guests gnaw their way, layer by layer, through camel to sheep to fish to fowl to the stewed dates buried like treasure and slick with the drippings from what's gone before.

This is the ultimate "one-pot" meal and I'm dying to try it. First of all, though, I am going to have to do for this Moorish feast what Julia Child did for French cooking: adapt it for the contemporary North American kitchen and palate. Quantities will have to be adjusted too, of course, as the dinner party for four hundred is a daunting undertaking for some.

Right off the bat I'm going to nix the camel packaging. The humps are apparently very fatty, and I have reservations about any beast whose best bits, according to the Roman emperor Heliogabalus, are the heels. Then there's the problem of bagging a bustard, which, in these parts at least, are as scarce as . . . well, plovers. No, the recipe will definitely require some creative noodling.

There is an updated version of the camel stuffathon that I could fall back on if pressed. It's called Turducken, a Cajun creation from southern Louisiana that involves the packing together of three kinds of fowl: chicken, duck and turkey. Each of these birds has to be deboned to start with, no simple task. Then they're pressed flat and layered, along with a variety of savory dressings, before being rolled up, trussed and slow-cooked—for twelve hours or more. Sounds like a lot of muss and fuss to me. I much prefer the Moors' stuff-it-as-it-comes methodology.

Homegrown lamb is always a big hit, so that seems a logical tradition to tap into for our purposes. But what to stuff it with? And what to stuff into the stuff that's got to get stuffed into all that other stuff along the way?

Tricky stuff. I suggest we assemble from the inside out.

Take one poppy seed. Using tweezers and a No. 001 drill bit, carefully insert the poppy seed into a mustard seed. Thus nested, the seeds can then be easily inserted into a caper. The caper can bed down inside a raisin, which will fit snugly inside a prune. A kiwi fruit, judiciously scooped, will accommodate the stuffed prune and it should be smooth stuffing from here on in. Kiwi into baby eggplant into jackfruit into guinea fowl into largemouth bass into rabbit into twenty-four-pound Butterball turkey—into the home stretch!

Position the fully packed and firmly trussed turkey inside the lamb. If desired, small items—garlic cloves, button mushrooms, toasted pine nuts, fish sticks (why not?)—may be added at this stage to fill up any unoccupied nooks and crannies. Pour two bottles of wine (preferably a robust red) into the mix, stir well and secure the stuffed lamb with sturdy kitchen twine. Dot with butter.

It may take a bit of jigging to stuff a stuffed lamb into a conventional oven, but I suggest you persevere. Otherwise you're looking at the hot-coals-in-a-backyard-pit routine, which is really more bother than it's worth. So heave-ho and away we go—into a 325° oven for 8 to 10 hours or until the lamb is pink and the fish sticks are nicely crisped.

Serve with mint sauce, mashed potatoes and a bowl of crème fraîche for when you get to the fruity centre. And please don't fight over the prune.

Another recipe for the books, Italian this time: spaghetti alla carbonara. It's a gem. And though it begs to be shared I don't suggest you should actually try to make something of it. Heaven forbid! It is offered up for your reading pleasure only.

It came my way from the Internet when I sent Google off on a search for the dish's origins. The recipe was in Italian, so when Google, so enthusiastic and ever obliging, offered to translate, I gratefully accepted. Here's what Google cooked up.

Spaghetti to the carbonara

spaghetti 450 g.

eggs 6

guanciale 180 g.

spinaci 200 g.

butter 20 g.

brodo of meat 100 cc.

$parmesan 70 g.

oil, knows them,

black pepper q.b.

Cut the guanciale listarelle thin and makes it you to go in little oil until is not very croccante, therefore taken the grease out of and you put an oil thread. You blink 4 egg yolks and two entire eggs with know them and pepper. You take a po' of eggs and of the guanciale, you add the brodo, frullate and passages to the chinois until obtaining one sauce. Fixed of sapore and density. Cuocete the spaghetti in salata water, drains them to you to the tooth, mantecateli with the rest of the eggs, guanciale and grattugiato $parmesan, therefore metteteli in the stampini it characterizes them imburra, lined to you with sbollentate leaves of spinaci. You put for a moment in furnace. Poured the sauce to the centre of the plate, giratevi the tortino of spaghetti and completed with fettine of raw guanciale and black pepper.

Google does not indicate how many people this will serve. No one is my guess. Still, this recipe is going into my Top Favourites file for sure, along with several other mystery dishes from the same chaotic kitchen: Pennette to the Angry One; Tortino of Zite Spugnole and in Kidskin Sauce; Spaghetti to the Guitar with Carciofi.

This silliness all started with an idle question over dinner. We were eating our carbonara, appreciative as always that something so good could be so simple. It's basically bacon and eggs and pasta with a hit of garlic and Parmesan. If you want to go the purist route you use the Italian salt-cured version of bacon, pancetta. That's what we do but it's tasty either way.

The question was: why is it called *carbonara?* Carbon is charcoal—a puzzling association. Our various books, which we explored while we ate, gave us some answers. But not all.

Spaghetti alla carbonara found its way to North America after World War II. When American soldiers were in Rome they would frequently avail themselves of local hospitality, accepting gratefully the food that came their way. But breakfast proved problematic. What the soldiers really hungered for was what they'd had back home: bacon and eggs. And their hosts were quick to oblige. Except that when bacon meets egg in Italy it's in a dish of pasta. Not exactly what the doctor ordered for the homesick G.I. but a fine, hearty meal nonetheless.

So far so good. But the origin of the name *carbonara* eluded us. So we googled it. The incomprehensible recipe was icing on the cake. Google had done its homework.

Carbonara got its name from the woodcutters who worked the forests in the Apennine region of Italy. Because they turned their harvest into charcoal they were called *carbonari*. A meal on the job would have to have been a simple one. Dried pasta, cheese and a lump of pancetta would have travelled well, and eggs were probably easily attainable from local farms. The carbonari used one other ingredient that is not as easily explained: lard. Why *lard?* Would fried pancetta not yield up adequate puddles of tasty grease? Did the farmer with the eggs have no olive oil to spare? Or butter? And what on earth would lard-laced pasta taste like? I can't imagine and Google didn't say.

We still have some googling to do. But it will have to wait. I'm still trying to figure out just how croccante my guanciale should be before I put it in the furnace.

Incidentally, spaghetti alla carbonara boasts such a rich history that the food writer Calvin Trillin has been promoting it for years as a replacement for the turkey at the American Thanksgiving meal. After all, he argues, it was not the pilgrims but the Italians—explorers like Columbus and Verrazzano—who were the first Europeans to set eyes on the New World.

I fully endorse Mr. Trillin's campaign. Not only does this pasta dish qualify for heritage status, there is no such thing as carbonara leftovers.

Here is our favourite recipe for spaghetti alla carbonara, a slightly modified version of the classic described in *The Fine Art of Italian Cooking* by Giuliano Bugialli. He delivers a brief lecture off the top: this dish, he tells us, is called "spaghetti with bacon and eggs on tourist menus." It is obvious that Mr. Bugialli does not think too highly of tourist menus because he continues with this stern warning: "Pancetta, of course, is not bacon, because it is not smoked; do not substitute bacon." He's absolutely right. But, if pushed, I cheat. What's a body to do when there's no pancetta in the house?

Spaghetti alla Carbonara

4 ounces pancetta, cut into small pieces

2 tablespoons olive oil

Pinch of hot chili flakes (This is optional, depending on the spiciness of your pancetta.)

Salt (optional)

1 large clove garlic, finely chopped

1 extra-large egg

⅓ cup freshly grated Parmesan cheese

1 tablespoon chopped parsley

½ pound spaghetti

Freshly ground black pepper

Bring the water for the spaghetti to a boil. In the meantime, in a small frying pan over low heat, slowly brown the pancetta in the oil along with the optional pepper flakes and salt. (I rarely use either. I find pancetta salty and spicy enough without them.) The pancetta should cook very, very slowly (about 15 minutes) so that all the fat is rendered out. When it is nearly crisp add the garlic, letting it cook until it is just beginning to colour. Remove from the heat.

226

While the pancetta is cooking, beat the egg lightly in a bowl and combine with the grated cheese and parsley.

When the pasta water reaches a boil, add some salt, cook the spaghetti until it is al dente, drain and place it in a large serving bowl. Add the contents of the frying pan and toss. Quickly, add the egg mixture and lots of freshly ground pepper, and toss some more. Serve hot.

Serves 2.

8

Travels with My Tummy

If you come to a fork in the road,
take it.

YOGI BERRA

Meals on Wheels

Our holiday home is a chocolate brown 1986 Volkswagen van. We call him Bruno. His various blemishes and abrasions are fondly referred to as liver spots. He runs out of breath on hills. And though he looks like a cracker box on wheels he is in fact a model of ingenious design and efficiency. Inside, every inch is used to practical purpose. There are closets and cupboards and smartly stacked shelves, all built in. The countertop swivels neatly into a table. Tucked away out of sight are a fridge, a stove, a tiny sink and a roomy fold-out double bed cum bench seat. And, as if this weren't luxury enough, Bruno's top pops up, revealing yet another bed beneath his sloping roof. Two regulation-size people, one bulky dog and, in a pinch, a couple of small children can cohabit comfortably for weeks in this craftily engineered space. Unfortunately, accommodating as he is, Bruno is not entirely reliable.

Vital organs fail. Parts fall off: the rearview mirror, a door handle and, on one memorable occasion, an entire door. The alternator fizzled in Nelson, B.C. The horn refused to honk on a mountain road during a precipitous descent into Bella Coola. But things went seriously downhill when, just four days into one particularly challenging camping holiday,

Bruno suffered a massive seizure and threw up all over Highway 93. At a place called Bummer's Flats.

It's a long haul from Bummer's Flats to just about anywhere else on Earth. Especially when you're sitting astride a gear lever thinking about corn. Four of us were wedged into the cab of the tow truck: me, Chris, Dexter the dog, and Norm from Wrench Bender Towing.

I was thinking about the corn, which was trapped in the van which was hitched to the tow truck, because it really should be cooked soon—today—if we were to get full value for the dollar we'd paid for it. But a corn roast seemed an unlikely diversion what with Bruno in emergency and us—where?

The only motel in town that would accept dogs and enable us to boil water for coffee was situated in what one guidebook called a "park-like" setting. The "park" being the slice of grass between the deep dust of the parking lot and a crusty, sour-smelling swamp. We were assigned to Unit 5. It was dark and cramped and as close to the highway as you could reasonably get without constituting a traffic hazard.

An added attraction was the railway yard, a mere stone's throw away, where freight cars lurched and screeched like bad-tempered giants in a punch-up. We wouldn't sleep, that was for certain. But we were determined to eat.

I asked our rent-a-car service rep for her recommendation. She directed us to the other end of town, to a Bavarian restaurant where, she assured us, the ribs were "to die for."

We settled the dog in front of the TV and aimed our rented Pontiac Sunfire in the direction of ribs and beer.

232

This particular little corner of Bavaria was tucked between the U-Decor-8 Home-Furnishing Depot and Action Equipment Rentals. We had a window table, which was nice as it afforded us a sweeping view of the baked concrete landscape, a kaleidoscope of winking neon and the four lanes of traffic blurring past.

The ribs were meaty and massive, the size of dinosaur bones. We gnawed our way through what we could and the rest were loaded into a Styrofoam carton—a rather extravagant doggie bag that convinced us that as long as we were incarcerated we would cook and eat "at home," in the perpetual twilight of Unit 5.

This was no picnic. The creaky infrastructure of Unit 5 demanded some delicately calibrated housekeeping manoeuvres. You could boil water, toast toast and cook yourself an egg. No problem. As long as you performed these operations sequentially. Any attempt at synchronicity instantly triggered a power outage. You also had to be very careful about *what* you cooked. Frying bacon, for example, would set off the smoke alarm, which could be silenced only by gouging out its bleating innards with a can opener wielded by a tall man with long arms standing on a bed astride a cowering dog.

While Bruno languished in intensive care waiting for his coolant-system transplant, our culinary odyssey continued. Eating out was out. Eating in was problematic. So we resorted to takeout and in the process discovered a dazzling, dizzying total-immersion food-shopping experience: the supermarket to beat all supermarkets. It was as huge and glitzy as a cruise ship, and we prowled the aisles like dumbstruck kids at a carnival. I wandered from the Hay-U-Ranch bread wagon to a giant lazy Susan stacked with baked-in-store double-chocolate fudge brownies. And ended up in Playland.

I was lined up behind a gaggle of six-year-olds waiting to play Nerf basketball when Chris tracked me down. It seemed there was another attraction I wouldn't want to miss. In produce.

I could hear thunder as we approached. A distant, muffled rumble. Then—a stuttering flash. Lightning? I looked up. Nothing. But then why should there be? We were in a supermarket, for heaven's sake! Then the rains came. A shower, really, that evaporated into mist almost immediately and settled like morning dew on the ranks of artfully arranged vegetables. Well, what do you know! A man-made, micro-managed, Disney-style weather system specially arranged to keep the carrots crisp and the shoppers on their toes.

Camping was never like this.

It seemed a lifetime before we tasted that special happiness again: felt the grit in our socks; drank real water from a real stream; cooked whatever we wanted whenever we wanted it without blowing a single fuse. And yes, got wet when it rained.

The corn, when we finally retrieved it, was done. Boiled in a bag in the heat of the sun, it was still the finest meal to come our way that week.

A reliable rule of thumb for the camping traveller is that the quality of food ingested deteriorates dramatically and in direct proportion to the number of miles logged. Discipline goes out the window. All things leafy or green or even remotely nutritious are off the menu. Junk food rules.

Things start out admirably enough. The larder is packed with salad fixings and fresh fruit and good, sturdy homemade bread. We have tubs of pasta sauce and lamb curry and just-laid eggs from my friend's pampered chickens. For a while we eat well, heads held high.

But inevitably, by about Day Five, we're running out of real food. We've left the land of plenty behind. There's not a butcher, a baker or an organic farmer in sight. Rest areas are so far apart we practise driving with our legs crossed.

So we settle for whatever we can get our hands on. Instant coffee. The occasional wizened potato. And bread that tastes of nothing at all. But mostly what we do is snack: potato chips, chocolate bars—Mars, Crispy Crunch, Skor. We eat cookies. We play Scrabble by lamplight with a pailful of bridge mixture between us. This is bad, really bad. But it gets worse. And it gets worse because an odd thing has happened: we're loving the fix we're in. We can't get enough of this terrible stuff. We've turned into a pair of mobile, bottomless dumpsters.

If Health Canada were to launch a rescue operation, if a barge loaded with fresh fruit and broccoli and wheat germ muffins appeared on the horizon, we would pelt it with jujubes and send it on its way. We adapt brilliantly to the rigours of life in the culinary badlands.

On one road trip I developed a deep and insistent craving

for tortilla chips. With tubs of salty, MSG-enhanced dip on the side. My favourite flavour was roasted garlic. It boasted thirty-four ingredients, stuff like propylene glycol alginate, monoesters and mono-diglycerides. There was a baba ghanouj concoction as well, another miracle of chemistry that kept me happily dipping for days.

One night we eat beet greens. This was purely accidental. They'd come attached to the beets that were the only vegetable on offer at the all-purpose general-store/laundromat/public-showers facility where we'd shopped. We've pretty much given up on vegetables. We prefer our food processed. We're at a crossroads and it's time to take stock.

Sensible folk for the most part, we eat wisely, cook lovingly and for the better part of the year are content with three nourishing meals a day. We don't eat what we can't pronounce. We never—well, hardly ever—fry our bread in bacon fat and we have played hundreds of games of cutthroat Scrabble without fuelling up on performance-enhancing chocolate-covered raisins.

At this stage in our journey, we know that if we are to kick the Twinkie habit we have only two options: we can forage for edible leaves, berries and seasonal fungi or we can head for the nearest population centre and pay for someone to cook us a decent meal.

One off-campground excursion took us to a heavily promoted restaurant near a bustling tourist centre an hour's drive away. The menu looked promising: pink scallops, mussels and clams in a marinara sauce; medallions of musk ox with a blueberry demi-glace; prawn brochettes dressed with a saffron-ginger aïoli; and fillet of ostrich.

"How does one fillet an ostrich?" Chris mused.

The woman who greeted us had a long face and wore black. When we asked for the wine list she sighed and said she'd see what she could do. Something must have come up, a death in the family perhaps. We never saw her again.

Our waiter materialized eventually and we asked him for the wine list. This he managed, on the run, making it absolutely clear that he was an extremely busy man and could we please stop asking him for things. He ground his teeth as he pried the cork from our overpriced bottle of Syrah.

Chris ordered the seafood in marinara sauce. He said it was okay. I ordered the sushi and sashimi appetizer. The sushi were the size of Big Macs and made, incredibly enough, with basmati rice. Undercooked basmati rice. They were very chewy. I picked out the slivers of raw carrot, ate the canned roe and left the rest.

The musk ox main course, Chris's choice, tasted very good indeed. Unfortunately, I opted for the special—bouillabaisse—curious to see if their interpretation of this classic in any way resembled the catch-as-catch-can facsimile I concoct at home. It didn't. But it had the charm of familiarity about it nonetheless. It was the seafood à la marinara appetizer craftily reincarnated as a main dish.

Any chef worth his salt will make innovative use of leftovers from the previous day. But this was an unprecedented turnaround. These were leftovers from a meal in progress! But wait—I do the chef an injustice. Further probing revealed one subtle adjustment: the broth had been graced with little chunks of salmon. Leftover, twice-cooked salmon, as it turned out. As tender and tasty as twice-cooked salmon is bound to be.

Chris, ever the optimist, ordered a parfait for dessert, a parfait in this case being a scoop of ice cream with fresh blackberries. Almost "parfait," but not quite. We did an initial exploratory to ferret out any traces of the previous course, but it was 100 percent musk ox free.

The next evening we had grilled hot dogs and warm beer at our picnic table under the trees. Tomorrow we would gather mushrooms and move on.

It was called a "summer kitchen" in the campground brochure. We liked the sound of that. It conjured up images, in watery pastels, of dappled light and gingham. Like something Monet might have arranged. We were lured from the beaten path to find out more.

But this was Needles, B.C., not Giverny, and though the ripe days of summer had long since passed, we loved what we saw nonetheless. This summer kitchen had no walls, just a sheltering roof, a dirt floor, two white plastic chairs and a plank table with a scarred oilcloth top. Dominating the shady space was the pièce de résistance: an old McClary Triumph wood-burning stove, cast iron, with yellowed enamel panels and an oven that, cold or hot, registered a permanent 350°F.

We were in luck. The tiny campground was empty and the summer kitchen was ours.

It sat in a grove of birch trees that tossed their leaves like gold coins at our feet. We could see the lake from here, beyond banks of bright chrysanthemums and past the grassy slope where a hundred fat and happy chickens puttered in the dusk. To the east the mountains rose like cardboard cutouts against a lilac sky. The place got ten out of ten for ambience. The food scored rather less: fried onions, potatoes boiled up with a few nub ends of carrot for interest, and corned beef.

The corned beef came from a can. Or, more precisely, it shot from the can, slipped through the chef's fingers and landed with a meaty splat in the grit and dust of the kitchen floor. The dog couldn't believe his good luck. Table scraps! Falling from the sky!

A minor scuffle ensued as we retrieved the meat course and, with a hearty ha-ha-not-to-worry, hosed it down at the water tap. After some judicious surgery it was ready for the frying pan, where, in its sodden state, it turned quickly to sludge amongst the (by now well-blackened) onions.

We called it Corned Beef Surprise. A curious cross between soup and hash, it nevertheless lent a certain textural interest to the potato-carrot combo that had morphed into porridge on the overstoked McClary Triumph. Our plastic tumblers were filled many times over with a young, very in-your-face red wine, and the whole lot was accompanied by selected readings from the tabloid press: *European Werewolves Succumb to Kennel Cough! Arab Sheik Proposes Marriage to Sexy Siamese Twins! Evil Boss Spikes Office Coffee with Laxatives!*

Dessert was one travel-worn pear and a Mars bar, divided with great care between the two of us.

Why do we do it? I wondered. Why do we—all us happy campers—forsake the shiny push-button conveniences of home to flail around in the bush, scrounging kindling and fetching water to concoct meals we'd never dream of inflicting on ourselves at home?

The reason, I suspect, aside from the accessibility of campgrounds and the unbeatable good value, is that we like who we become when we are there. We peel off our city skin to walk in the rain and read by lantern light and drink from cupped hands straight from a stream. We eat when we're hungry and put ketchup on our eggs. We're like kids at play in a free space where no rules apply because out here under the sky there's no one around to scold us but the chipmunks.

So what if there's sand in the butter and the salt won't pour? Perhaps what we discover in our kitchen-in-the-woods is that happiness has really nothing whatsoever to do with having it easy. Or having it all. What you remember at the end of the day is the smell of sizzling bacon in the morning air, that last sip of wine beneath the stars and how impossibly good it all tasted.

I was ruminating on this and the heady prospect of tomorrow's breakfast—eggs over easy and recycled Surprise—when Chris rose from his chair, lifted his glass over the debris of dinner and proposed this toast:

"To Al Fresco," he said, "the inventor of the summer kitchen."

The Maine Event

Homeland Security was not part of the American lexicon when we had our brush with the Secret Service back in 1985. Just as well. My behaviour, definitely suspect then, would be an indictable offence today.

The Incident, which I'm sure is how it's referred to in the files, occurred at Mabel's Lobster Claw, a restaurant on the beach road near Kennebunkport, Maine. Mabel's, we were told, was a favourite haunt of the then vice-president, George Bush, who lived on one of the sprawling multi-million-dollar properties nearby.

Mabel's sat in the lap of this crushed velvet landscape like a fly in a bowl of vichyssoise. Its roof hung like a hammock over a haphazard arrangement of what looked like tar paper and reclaimed pilings. Intrigued, we reserved a table for dinner that night—the last one, Mabel was at pains to point out, as the restaurant was otherwise fully booked for a private party.

We were there at seven. There were very few cars in the lot but one caught our eye: a very shiny black stretch limo with tinted windows. A lot of men were standing around smoking cigarettes and observing our approach. We pulled up beside the limo and got out.

I react badly to limos in general, over-stretched, over-dressed limos in particular. And this one was enormous, heavy with chrome and gloomy as a hearse.

"Yuck," I said, and pressed my face against a window to see inside.

The men moved out of the shadows. I grinned and wished them a good evening, noticing for the first time that they were all wearing hearing aids.

"Deaf," I whispered to Chris. "It must be a convention."

I chirruped "Good evening" again, louder this time so they could hear. They followed us inside.

The dining room was full. A party of a dozen or more occupied one large table. The hearing-challenged men were escorted to another, and Chris and I were seated nearby. I noticed three things. Despite the summer heat, the men all wore raincoats. They drank lemonade. And when they spoke, which was rarely, they did so very, very quietly.

"Maybe they're not deaf," I ventured. "Or else they're very adept at reading lips."

Then we spied George Bush. He was presiding over the large table on the far side of the dining room. He wore one of those white V-necked tennis sweaters with a lizard on it. In fact everybody swooning around him wore a white tennis sweater with a lizard on it.

I thought this extremely funny, but Chris's attention was elsewhere. His eyes rolled wildly in the direction of the big men in raincoats. He was trying to speak without moving his lips.

"They're Secret Service men!" he hissed. "And those aren't hearing aids. They're wired!"

I snuck a peek. This was undoubtedly the case. And it was thrilling! Because if they were wired then we were bugged! It was just like in the movies.

Mabel came to take our order. We tried to behave normally, like the innocent tourists we were, but it's odd what happens to your composure when you're under surveillance. We were strangers, after all. And we were looking decidedly fidgety, as if "We'll both have steamed lobster, please" was code for "There's a bomb in my knapsack so you better watch out."

A small vase of cut flowers sat on the table between us. My Birkenstock connected with Chris's shin.

"The microphone"—I mouthed the words—"it's in the flowers."

We talked about the weather with the determined jollity of two-bit actors with a crummy script.

I don't know what got into me then to make me do what I did. I have a perverse streak that compels me to unspeakable acts of defiance, like pinching the produce and driving on the shoulder when I'm explicitly instructed not to do so. *I dare you* means *do it* and I did.

I picked up the vase of flowers, brought it close to my mouth and delivered a garbled rant about privacy and presumption of innocence and paranoid delusions and how "this kind of thing would never happen where we come from."

Chris went an alarming shade of grey. But the men with wires were sucking on lobster claws and paying us no heed whatsoever. Puzzled, I examined the flower arrangement more closely.

"Testing . . . testing . . ."

Mabel arrived with our lobsters. She was watching me closely.

243

"I'm just testing. You know. To see if they're real."

"Uh-huh."

"They are." I smiled brightly. I replaced the vase and tucked my lobster bib around my neck. "We're from Canada."

She smiled, satisfied. That, it would seem, explained everything.

Or maybe not. We've not been back that way since then, and I'm not all that confident about our welcome if we did. They've got my name—I made the reservation. I made disparaging noises about the vice-president's silly car. And I was engaged in some sort of subversive activity with a flower vase. It's all a bit dicey, really. I'll probably confine my travels to Canada from here on in. Besides, I can always find lobster back home in Nova Scotia.

Son Bich!
The Chef Has Twelve Toes!

My idea of a perfect mid-February holiday is to head for the sun, loll about on a tropical beach and eat myself silly. And no one does silly better than the Dominicans.

Dining out in the Dominican Republic is the stuff of high farce, a bit like being trapped in a Denny's with Basil Fawlty at the helm. It's difficult to pick a clear winner in what we dubbed the Silly Meal contest. There were so many.

I've therefore winnowed down the top contenders into two categories. Silly Meals that offered top value for the peso, and Even Sillier Meals that we'll eventually pay for when we've renegotiated our overdraft privileges with our bank manager.

The Best-Value-for-Silliness award goes to an open-air shack on the beach in the small town of Las Galeras. We had fled there after sampling the food at one of the nearby hotels: "baked" turkey roll, which had actually been baked several times over; canned gravy; and a side of soft yellow broccoli. Tang was the highlight at breakfast.

What we really wanted was simple Dominican fare: fresh fish and local fruit. The lean-to on the beach promised both.

We were shown to the "patio" seating—a picnic table set up on the sand under a big silver moon and a sky full of stars. We were grateful for the moon. Our dining spot, as well as having no name, had no electricity. Chris, anticipating the problem, had brought a flashlight.

Inside, under a pitched roof of thatch and corrugated tin, a group of about twenty bustled about in the dark, doing we couldn't imagine what as there was no one to feed but ourselves and we hadn't ordered yet. It looked like a family enterprise: a little girl with pink hair ribbons washed dishes at a big plastic tub. A young man with his two small sons appeared to be in charge of a roughed-in booth that served as a bar. Their bailiwick also included the sound system—a rusted-out blue Toyota pick-up parked, doors flung wide and radio blaring, a few feet from our table.

The music provided a powerful incentive to drink, and a hand-lettered menu nailed on the bar listed our options.

There were the familiar old standbys like piña colada and Cuba libre. But after that came a list of offerings that even our trusty Berlitz phrase book couldn't help us with: *Frup ponch. Ron sawer. Son bich.* Son bich? We read on.

There were two options involving what we guessed to be gin: *jin toni* or *yin toninc.* And, improbably enough, a *daykiri.* We ordered beer.

Our waitress, a young woman in a Blue Jays jacket, rummaged through a picnic cooler in the shadows behind us. She appeared with the dinner offerings laid out on a platter: one chubby pink snapper and a good-size langouste, which is a spiny, or rock, lobster. Marvellous! We ordered both. Our tummies did happy little somersaults in anticipation.

The bustle at the back of the shack took on new urgency. People leaped into action over a small clay barbecue and the bartender/DJ team raced to the pick-up to punch up the decibels.

Time passed. The moon ducked behind the clouds and we were now in the deepest dark. Sand fleas munched on our ankles, and the local beach dogs had begun to manoeuvre themselves into position around our table. They looked like long-legged Chihuahuas with hungry brown eyes.

We ordered two more beers, a fortuitous move as the drinks team, evidently bored with the gringo clientele, was now dismantling the bar and loading it into the back of the pick-up. It eventually lurched off into the night, dragging a muffler and a wailing Bob Marley in its wake.

All activity around the barbecue had suddenly come to a full stop. Everyone was standing around drinking Pepsi.

After a while our waitress materialized out of the gloom.

She'd just remembered something. Would we be wanting *patatas*? Or *arroz*? The timing seemed ominous. Our fish, surely, had long since been cooked. We were very hungry. We decided on *patatas*.

Another flurry erupted in the vicinity of the cookstove. The *patatas* brigade had obviously been caught unawares.

We scratched our ankles and waited. A truck pulled up, the driver got out and, in the light of his headlamps, began setting up racks of clothes on the sand: blouses, blue jeans, denim skirts, men's shirts. Now we had a travelling flea market just feet from where we sat, and the entire staff appeared to have abandoned the kitchen and gone shopping.

We peered into the shack to see what, if anything, was happening on the *patatas* front and were reassured to note that Grandad had been left in charge and was hard at work over a frying pan. It was quite late by now, and the dogs, discouraged, had ambled off in search of better pickings. We regretted not having ordered a son bich when we'd had the chance.

About three-quarters of the way toward the bottom of our second beer, we realized that the flea market crowd had now reassembled in an anxious knot around Grandad and his frying pan. There was a sudden kerfuffle as various helpers stumbled about in the dark in search of plates and, presumably, our by-now-overcooked fish.

When dinner arrived we suppressed the impulse to applaud.

The langouste was marvellous. The snapper, crackling-crisp on the outside and tender as butter on the inside, was indescribably delicious. Neither were hot. But the fried *patatas,* cooked to a turn by Grandad, were. We ate by flashlight.

The bill came, scribbled on a scrap of cardboard—1,800 pesos, about $20 Canadian. An unbeatable bargain. But the silliness quotient was to escalate rapidly in the days that followed.

The best meals of all were plucked from the ocean where we happened to be wandering at the time. On one particularly spectacular beach, which, at high noon, appeared to be ours and ours alone, we were approached by an elderly man with a sweet smile offering lunch. He was all set up, he said. Our table, if we wanted it, was ready. And he led us to a clearing in the palm grove by the sea. Our table was, as usual, a jerry-rigged affair and the menu a limited one: fresh sea bass grilled over an open fire, a platter of rice from the local paddies, cold beer and a salad of marinated shredded cabbage.

We spent a happy hour picking away at this impromptu feast with plastic forks and exchanging vocabulary, English to Spanish and back again, with our amiable barefoot chef, who sat protectively by our side batting off the flies with a palm frond.

The pivotal moment came when he directed our attention to his feet, raising them with shy pride to a vantage point just inches from our cabbage salad.

"Doce," he said. Twelve. He had twelve toes. Six on each foot. We were suitably amazed.

An exceptionally tasty lunch, with a Spanish lesson and an intimate encounter with native anatomy thrown in, was only mildly silly and cost us less than $20.

Cas'a Papon in Las Terranas delivered a very different lunch experience. It was a charming spot, a tiny beach hut filled with happy chatter and seductive smells. We spent our first lunchtime visit there lusting after the spread at a neighbouring table. They'd ordered crab—a monster crab with claws like paddles. We paid little attention to what we ate, so intent were we on what we'd missed. We cornered the proprietor afterwards and made arrangements to be served a similar feast two days later.

We should have anticipated the folly of what we'd done. For one thing, we rarely eat crab. Mainly because it isn't lobster. And besides, I'm always amazed at how little meat there really is in that capacious shell. The other consideration we so blithely overlooked was how much this indulgence was going to cost.

Our personal Cas'a Papon crab weighed in at nearly four pounds. The claws had been detached and cracked open with a bamboo truncheon and the whole thing sprawled on a platter of such enormous proportions that there was scarcely room on the table for the bottle of Chilean wine we'd ordered to accompany it.

We pried the sweet, steaming meat from the claws. It was delicious. Which was just as well, as that was the only meat to be had. A thorough search of the massive crater that was the body of the beast revealed little else that was edible. It had been scraped clean and stuffed with something we couldn't identify. It had the texture of pâté and tasted faintly of the sea. But it wasn't crab. We stared gloomily at the ravaged carcass and drank our wine. That was our other mistake.

One should never drink wine, certainly not cheap wine, on an empty stomach in the high heat of a tropical noon. The brain disengages. You find yourself peeling off wads of soggy pesos and handing them to complete strangers with barely a whimper. Our four-ounce crab lunch, with wine, cost nearly $80. We scuttled back to our hotel and fell asleep.

"Everyone should dine at La Puntilla de Piergiorgo (in the tourist town of Sosua) at least once," said our guidebook. So off we went. The place was spectacular. Spectacular in the way a three-ring circus or a ten-billion-dollar replica of the *Titanic* is spectacular. The terraced open-air dining area was the size of two football fields. Tables were snugged into individual balconies on a cliff overlooking the sea. Fairy lights winked from the palm trees.

We arrived without reservations. The mâitre d' raised an eyebrow, shot a dubious glance at my Reeboks, sighed and showed us to a table.

What followed remains somewhat of a blur. Servers came and went, battalions of them, emerging from the shadows with complimentary apéritifs, wedges of bruschetta and long-stemmed roses for "the lady." There were beer waiters, pepper mill waiters, water waiters and wine stewards. There were people to brush away crumbs and wipe your chin and check to make sure your enjoyment level remained at a fever pitch.

Piergiorgo himself oiled his way to our table, caressed my neck and made earnest inquiries as to our health and appetites. He wore what looked like white polyester pajamas and a tipsily angled toupée.

The silliness quotient rose sharply at the dessert stage, when I made the mistake of ordering bananas flambé. A young man whose name tag identified him as Buffalo Bill rolled up to our table with a trolley full of incendiary equipment. A hush descended on the fairy-lit acreage as the bananas were flung into a pan, tossed about, then doused with brandy and set alight. Bill then set to work on our coffee, pouring it from glass to glass in great flaming blue arcs. After which, he washed his hands in brandy and set them alight as well.

The final presentation included a complimentary hand mirror stamped with Piergiorgo's autograph for me and the bill for the gentleman.

I won't tell you how much all this hilarity cost. Let's just say the joke was on us.

The Air Meals Reward Plan

Dinner is being served. It's not a pretty sight and I'm taking notes. An extremely large woman with a pesky cough and a jumbo-size bag of Werthers toffee is seated on my right. To my left is a man who, from the corner of my eye, looks alarmingly like Alberta premier Ralph Klein. Ralph Klein would not, under any circumstances imaginable, be my No. 1 pick as a dinner companion. But I'm in no position to table hop. We're trapped here, cheek to cheek to cheek so to speak, in a blue-ceilinged corridor of cumulus clouds 33,000 feet above Winnipeg. It's Hospitality Service time on flight 124.

You may not be familiar with this concept: "in-flight meals." Or the terms "hospitality" and "service" either, come to think of it. This is the stuff of a long-gone era in airline travel. None of what follows could possibly happen today.

The pretzels come first, then drinks. We nibble and sip, testing the intricate elbow-to-elbow choreography that will see us through the dinner hour with as few collisions as possible. The woman's cough tends to throw her off stride. And Ralph Klein's snack-retrieval routine is complicated by the need to juggle, along with a handful of slippery pretzels, a set of headphones, several pounds of newsprint and a can of beer. (It's probably not Klein at all, I decide. The real Ralph Klein would be ensconced up front, beyond the blue curtain, with all the precious extra inches business-class money can buy.)

For dinner we are given a choice of chicken, lasagna or vegetarian.

"Vegetarian?" I ask. "Could you be more specific?"

"It's a sort of vegetable dish," explains the flight attendant.

I'm hungry. I opt for lasagna. And a baby-size bottle of chilled red wine.

Both my dinner companions are now cocooned with headphones, plugged in to a movie that features a man in a tux being chased through city streets by several thousand women in wedding gowns. I leave them to it and turn my attention to the marvels of culinary minimalism laid out beneath the see-through roof of my dinner tray.

The salad, assembled with tweezer-tip precision, sits primly in a bowl the size of an eggcup: yellow lettuce, two slices of cucumber, a pinch of shredded carrot and a sprinkling of Styrofoam packing pellets cleverly disguised as croutons. I eat anyway, grateful for the dressing that comes in a specially sealed child-proof thimble-pack from Kraft, and press on.

There's a woolly bun the size of a tennis ball, a swab of fluffy butter and a postcard-size platter of what has been billed as lasagna. It doesn't look anything like lasagna. It looks like cream of tomato soup. I fish about with my fork and manage to snare two four-inch lengths of noodle. So far so good. I prod some more, trolling hungrily for a hint of meat however tiny, a thread of cheese of any kind. I settle for tomato-noodle soup.

The wine goes down like Kool-Aid. I eye the dessert, which, though a riot of colour—red, pink and a violent, sulphurous yellow—is otherwise unidentifiable. Applying my soup fork with surgical precision, I pry off the red skin on top. Oh goody. Cherry Jell-O. The bottom layer is the Hospitality Service version of cake. And sandwiched between is pink foam that tastes rather like Pepto-Bismol. It is a poor accompaniment to red wine. I opt for the wine. And while I sip I hatch a plan.

It's basically a rewards plan, with a twist: the idea would be to compensate the victims of the kinds of food crimes that I've just described. Instead of air *miles* you'd earn air *meals*,

253

accumulating points for every flaccid salad, every unadorned ribbon of rubber lasagna, every chemically enhanced mystery dessert you manage to choke down. You could then cash in your nausea points for something edible next time round. I'm thinking picnics here. Attractively packed, gingham-wrapped, in returnable carry-on lap-top wicker baskets. Offerings would vary. There would be a Budget Basket for starters, something simple like a plough-man's lunch—a wedge of nippy cheese, good bread, a bottle of Guinness and a mouth-puckering pickled onion. Frequent Eaters would be able to trade up quickly to high-end snacks like smoked salmon with capers, venison pâté, tapenade, sweet ripe figs and—why not?—your own personal pocket-size, single-swig flask of fine French brandy.

And our slogan? How about—*Air meals: the worse they get, the better you fare.* I love it! But will it fly?

The End . . .

According to the ancient Mayans the world is scheduled to end on December 23, 2012. That doesn't leave a lot of time to plan my last meal. And surely a slap-up dinner is in order on the eve of such a momentous occasion.

I decided I would have mine a few months early, in August of 2012, to avoid the last-meal rush. Besides, I would want to hold it outdoors. The place I have in mind is a sunny meadow, the property of friends, not far from where I live. It's a magical place. By summer's end the meadow grass is waist high and in the evening light the distant hills turn smoky blue. Bonny the horse lives here, and from time to time she holds court as neighbouring folk, bearing platters of food and flagons of homemade wine, troop to her back-yard to party. If we want to make hay while the sun shines, I can't think of a more beautiful place to do it.

In the middle of the meadow is a stand of ancient walnut trees. I would set up picnic tables in their leafy shade and string lanterns from their boughs. Some of us would bring binoculars so we could watch the birds as we eat. And we would all bring our dogs, who would chase the horse who would cavort through the meadow egging them on.

I would surround myself with a few special friends, but mostly it would be family, several dozen at last count, and I would fly them in—from England and New York and Washington and Texas and points across Canada. We're going to need a lot of picnic tables. And a fire pot or two to cook things on: oil drums will do the trick, with racks on top for cooking pots. And because this is an occasion of immense import we would probably see fit to shuck our mucky boots and blue jeans in favour of long skirts and big hats and freshly pressed shirts. We would look quite grand in our end-of-the-world finery as we file, skirts gathered high, through the deep grass to our feast beneath the trees.

The tables would be set with bright linen, flowers and the finest china we could scrounge. The champagne would be iced and ready. We'd pop corks and pass the salad—home-grown greens, sweet cherry tomatoes and a sprinkling of nasturtium petals. We'd help ourselves to hunks of fresh-baked bread, dense and chewy, with lots of butter. Then we'd open the wine, a once-in-a-lifetime wine—an '83 Côte Rôtie, if we're lucky—poured with generous abandon and consumed with gusto because there's lots more where that came from.

Then what? I want fish, a modest portion before the main event, which will likely come from the sea as well. I think I'd choose mackerel to start, smoked, from the cold waters off the coast of England. I'd have a sharp horseradish cream sauce to accompany it.

After that, wild mushrooms: chanterelles would be nice if we could find some early ones. We'd be too late for our local morels but possibly, with money being no object, we would have fresh porcini flown in specially from Italy. They'd be as big as dinner plates and grilled like steaks.

For the main course I would have lobster. Nova Scotia lobster, boiled, with drawn butter and lemon. I will have as many as I can eat, which might be many indeed. And so what if their juices run down our chins and onto the front of our special last-meal dresses? It wouldn't matter.

I would want a platter of vegetables as well, whatever the garden yields—steamed green beans and buttered parsnips and red-skinned potatoes boiled up with plenty of garlic.

We would, I suspect, be feeling quite full by now, so we'd sit back as the sun dipped behind the hills and listen as the frogs began their rusty squawk in the damp grass by the pond. We'd talk. About inconsequential things—how good everything tasted, and the books we'd read, and if perhaps it would be appropriate to pour just a bit more wine.

It would be. And we do. By now, the children would be squirming in their seats and, having passed up the unfamiliar treat of lobster, clamouring for dessert.

I'll make clafouti. And pick the blackberries to go in it. Maybe my friend Annie would bake us a cake, her famous-in-these-parts chocolate beet cake would do very nicely indeed. We might need several. Topped with generous dollops of whipped cream. Or—even better—mascarpone.

This would be followed by nuts (walnuts, as they're free for the taking) and cheese: Saint Agur and a blue Wensleydale. I'll have to make a special trip to England for the Wensleydale. It's not to be found anywhere else, a discovery I made after I first encountered it fifteen years ago.

I think a splash of Calvados would go well about now. It's dark. The children are slumped in their mothers' laps, asking when can they go home and is it time yet for a bedtime story.

Eventually, when the moon is high in the sky, we'd turn out the lanterns and head through the fields for home. There would be no talk of washing up, not tonight. And no one feels the need to say goodbye. There's always tomorrow, after all. And December seems a long, long time away.

Permissions

Chapter 1

Page 7: quote by A. J. Liebling reprinted from *Between Meals*, by permission of Russell & Volkening Inc.

Page 14: recipe ("Blueberry Grunt") from *Out of Old Nova Scotia Kitchens*, by Marie Nightingale, reprinted by permission of Nimbus Publishing Ltd.

Chapter 2

Page 43: quote by Jane Grigson from *The Mushroom Feast*, reprinted by permission of the publisher, Alfred A. Knopf Inc.

Page 59: quote from *The Physiology of Taste*, by J. A. Brillat-Savarin (translation by M. F. K. Fisher), reprinted by permission of the publisher, Random House Inc.

Chapter 3

Page 81: quote (James Beard "Appreciation") from *The Art of Eating*, by M. F. K. Fisher. Copyright © 1990, publisher Macmillan Ltd.

Page 95–96: quotes from *The Encyclopedia of Fish Cookery*, by A. J. McClane. Copyright © 1977 by A. J. McClane and Arie DeZanger. Reprinted by permission of Henry Holt and Company, LLC

Chapter 4

Page 121–122: excerpts from "Soon you could eat all you like," by John Saunders, reprinted with permission of *The Globe and Mail*

Page 124–126: quotes from *The Physiology of Taste*, by J. A. Brillat-Savarin (translation by M. F. K. Fisher), reprinted by permission of the publisher, Random House Inc.

Page 126: quote by M. F. K. Fisher from *The Art of Eating*. Copyright © 1990, publisher Macmillan Ltd.

Chapter 5

Page 136: excerpts from the *Independent on Sunday*, reprinted by permission of the author, Terry Durack

Page 138: quote from *The Man Who Ate Everything*, by Jeffrey Steingarten, reprinted by permission of the publisher, Random House Inc.

Page 140: quote ("Sweetbreads," p. 773, 43 words) reprinted from *The Oxford Companion to Food*, by Alan Davidson (1999), by permission of Oxford University Press

Page 143: recipe ("Haggis") from *Out of Old Nova Scotia Kitchens*, by Marie Nightingale, reprinted by permission of Nimbus Publishing Ltd.

Page 149: excerpts ("Marmite") from the *Guardian*, reprinted by permission of the author, Laura Barton

Page 152: quote ("Tapioca," p. 782, 23 words) reprinted from *The Oxford Companion to Food*, by Alan Davidson (1999), by permission of Oxford University Press

Page 157: quote from *The Fran Lebowitz Reader*, by Fran Lebowitz, by permission of the publisher, Random House Inc.

Chapter 6

Page 161: quote by Erma Bombeck from *Motherhood: The Second Oldest Profession*, by Erma Bombeck, reprinted by permission of the Aaron M. Priest Literary Agency

Page 170: quote by Bennett Cerf from *Bubble and Squeak*, by John Goode, reprinted by permission of the publisher, Lothian Books, 1987

Page 170–171: quotes from *The Rituals of Dinner*, copyright © 1991, by Margaret Visser. Reprinted by permission of the publisher, Harper-Collins Publishers Ltd.

Page 178: quote ("Marmalade," p. 481, 19 words) from *The Oxford Companion to Food*, by Alan Davidson (1999), by permission of Oxford University Press

Chapter 7

Page 208: quote by Jane Grigson from *The Vegetable Book*, reprinted by permission of the publisher, Alfred A. Knopf Inc.

Page 214: recipe ("Prairie Oyster") from *The Art of Eating*, by M. F. K. Fisher. Copyright © 1990, publisher Macmillan Ltd.

Page 219: recipe ("Baked Camel") from *Water Music*, by T. Coraghessan Boyle. Copyright © 1981 by T. Coraghessan Boyle. By permission of Little, Brown and Co., Inc.